Grade **3**

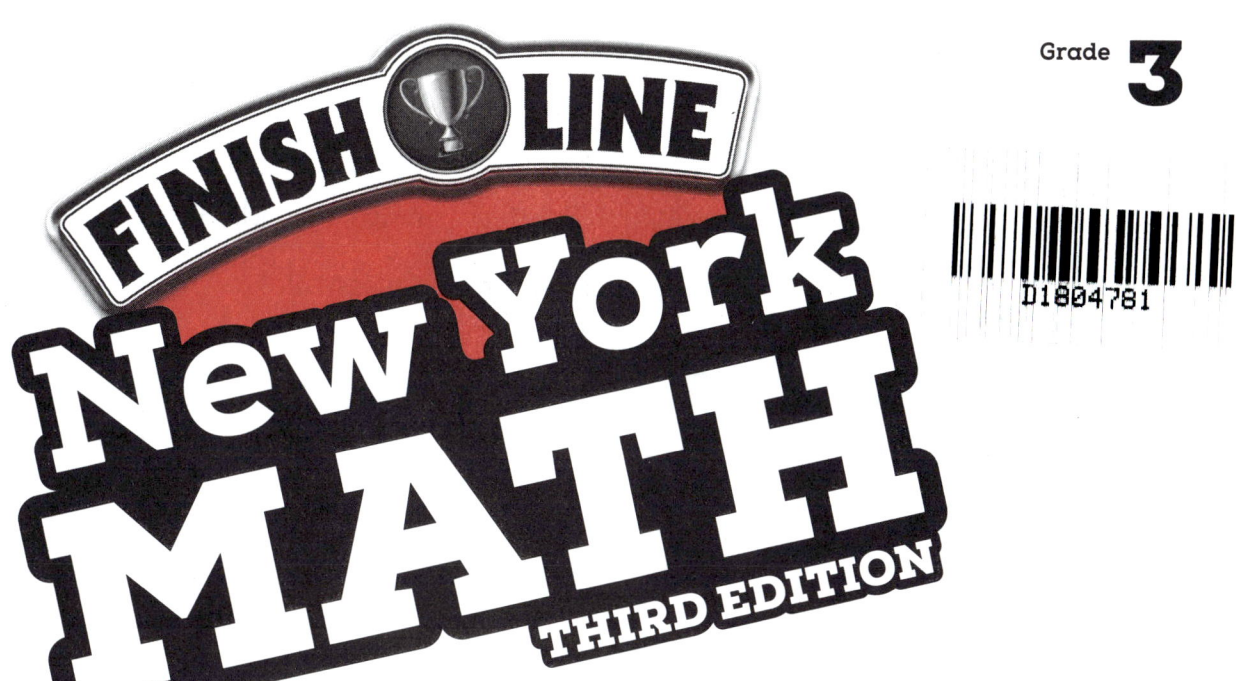

Illustrations: Laurie Conley, Michael Fink, Marty Husted, Harry Norcross

Photos: United States coin images from the United States Mint

ISBN 978-0-8454-7901-8

Copyright © 2015 The Continental Press, Inc.

No part of this publication may be reproduced in any form or by any means, electronic, mechanical, photocopying, recording, or otherwise, without the prior written permission of the publisher. All rights reserved. Printed in the United States of America.

TABLE OF CONTENTS

About Finish Line New York Math ... **5**

UNIT 1: Big Ideas from Grade 2 ... **7**

LESSON 1	2.NBT.5, 7	**Adding Two- and Three-Digit Numbers** [connects to 3.NBT.2]	**8**
LESSON 2	2.NBT.5, 7	**Subtracting Two- and Three-Digit Numbers** [connects to 3.NBT.2]	**15**
LESSON 3	2.MD.1	**Measuring Length** [connects to 3.MD.4]	**23**
LESSON 4	2.G.2	**Tiling Rectangles** [connects to 3.MD.7.a, c]	**29**
LESSON 5	2.G.1	**Polygons** [connects to 3.G.1]	**37**
		UNIT 1 REVIEW	**44**

UNIT 2: Operations and Algebraic Thinking, Part 1 ... **51**

LESSON 6	3.OA.1	**Understanding Multiplication**	**52**
LESSON 7	3.OA.5	**Properties of Multiplication**	**59**
LESSON 8	3.OA.2	**Understanding Division**	**66**
LESSON 9	3.OA.6	**Connecting Multiplication and Division**	**73**
LESSON 10	3.OA.4, 7	**Multiplication Facts**	**79**
LESSON 11	3.OA.4, 7	**Division Facts**	**86**
LESSON 12	3.OA.9	**Patterns**	**92**
		UNIT 2 REVIEW	**99**

UNIT 3: Number and Operations in Base Ten ... **105**

LESSON 13	3.NBT.1	**Rounding Whole Numbers**	**106**
LESSON 14	3.NBT.2	**Adding Whole Numbers**	**113**
LESSON 15	3.NBT.2	**Subtracting Whole Numbers**	**120**
LESSON 16	3.NBT.3	**Multiplying by Multiples of Ten**	**127**
		UNIT 3 REVIEW	**133**

UNIT 4: Operations and Algebraic Thinking, Part 2 ... **138**

LESSON 17	3.OA.3	**One-Step Word Problems with Multiplication and Division**	**139**
LESSON 18	3.OA.8	**Two-Step Word Problems**	**146**
		UNIT 4 REVIEW	**155**

UNIT 5: Number and Operations—Fractions — **160**

LESSON 19	3.NF.1	Understanding Fractions	**161**
LESSON 20	3.NF.2.a, b	Fractions on a Number Line	**168**
LESSON 21	3.NF.3.a, b, c	Equivalent Fractions	**175**
LESSON 22	3.NF.3.d	Comparing Fractions	**182**
		UNIT 5 REVIEW	**189**

UNIT 6: Measurement and Data — **195**

LESSON 23	3.MD.1	Time	**196**
LESSON 24	3.MD.1	Solving Problems with Time	**203**
LESSON 25	3.MD.2	Liquid Volume	**210**
LESSON 26	3.MD.2	Mass	**217**
LESSON 27	3.MD.3	Picture Graphs	**224**
LESSON 28	3.MD.3	Bar Graphs	**232**
LESSON 29	3.MD.4	Measurement Data on Line Plots	**241**
LESSON 30	3.MD.5.a, b; 6	Understanding Area	**249**
LESSON 31	3.MD.7.a, b	Multiplying to Find Area	**256**
LESSON 32	3.MD.7.c, d	Adding to Find Area	**263**
LESSON 33	3.MD.8	Perimeter and Area	**271**
		UNIT 6 REVIEW	**279**

UNIT 7: Geometry — **287**

LESSON 34	3.G.1	Plane Figures and Polygons	**288**
LESSON 35	3.G.1	Quadrilaterals	**295**
LESSON 36	3.G.2	Partitioning Shapes	**302**
		UNIT 7 REVIEW	**309**

Glossary — **314**

Flash Cards — **321**

About Finish Line New York Math

Finish Line New York Math, Third Edition, will help you prepare for math tests. Each year in math class, you learn new skills and ideas. You build on the math skills you already have; you prepare to learn new math skills in the future. As your mathematics knowledge grows, it is important to master the concepts you learn each year. Then you will better understand the ideas you will learn next year.

This book is divided into units of related lessons. Each lesson concentrates on one main math idea. The lesson reviews things you have learned in math class. Each lesson is broken into four parts.

❶ Introduction

The Introduction of each lesson reviews the math skill. It provides explanations and examples. It reviews important math vocabulary. You may see pictures and diagrams to help you understand the skill.

❷ Focused Instruction

The Focused Instruction part guides you through two or more practice problems. First, you will read the problem. Then you will work through a series of questions to help you find the answer. Sometimes the instructions will ask you to work with a partner. As you work through the problem, you will practice the skills you need to understand the main idea of the lesson. There are hints and reminders along the sides of the pages to help you remember what you have learned. At the end of the Focused Instruction, you will do one to three additional problems; these problems do not have hints.

❸ Guided Practice

The third part is Guided Practice, where you will work alone to complete two to three problems. These problems are open-ended, which means you have to write the answer. You may have to show your work, make a graph, draw a diagram, or do some other mathematical task. Again, there will be hints and reminders to help you out.

Part 4 Independent Practice

Finally, you will complete the Independent Practice. You will work by yourself to complete two to three pages of questions. These questions will be a variety of item types. In addition to multiple-choice and open-ended questions, you will also do multiple-choice items with more than one correct answer. You may need to fill in a table with information or complete a sentence or equation. Always look carefully at the question to decide the correct way to answer it. You may not be familiar with all the question types. Ask questions if you do not understand. The Independent Practice does not have any hints or reminders. You must use everything you learned in the first three parts to complete this section.

At the end of each unit is a unit review. In the review, you will use all the skills you worked on in that unit. You will see different item types, just like in the Independent Practice section. There will not be any hints or reminders.

A glossary and a set of flash cards appear at the end of the book. The glossary contains important words and terms along with their definitions from the book. The flash cards will help you review important ideas, formulas, and symbols from the book. There are some blank flash cards, too. You can use these to make flash cards for the things you most need to work on.

Developing your math skills will help you as you continue to learn and will allow you to use math in your everyday life.

UNIT 1
Big Ideas from Grade 2

In grade 2, you learned how to compare numbers. You also solved word problems, measured length, and recognized shapes. Now you can use what you know about numbers and shapes to work with two- and three-digit numbers, measure objects, and understand polygons.

LESSON 1 Adding Two- and Three-Digit Numbers In this lesson, you will add numbers with two or three digits.

LESSON 2 Subtracting Two- and Three-Digit Numbers In this lesson, you will subtract numbers with two or three digits, using regrouping when necessary.

LESSON 3 Measuring Length In this lesson, you will measure or estimate length using different measuring instruments and units, such as inches, feet, or yards.

LESSON 4 Tiling Rectangles In this lesson, you will use tiling to find the area of rectangles.

LESSON 5 Polygons In this lesson, you will identify different types of polygons and practice drawing these shapes.

LESSON 1

Adding Two- and Three-Digit Numbers

CCLS: 2.NBT.5, 7

Part 1 Introduction

To **add** means to combine to find a total. You can add in different ways. One way is to use place value.

A worker is stacking boxes. He has stacked 23 boxes. He needs to add 14 more boxes. How many will he stack in all?

Use place-value blocks to show 23.

Use place-value blocks to show 14.

Then combine the blocks. There are 3 tens blocks and 7 ones blocks. There is 37 in all.

You can stack numbers to add them. Line up the numbers by place value. Add the ones, then the tens. Then add the hundreds.

```
          Tens
 Hundreds  |  Ones
    ↓      ↓    ↓
    5      1    3
  + 2      4    6
  ─────────────────
    7      5    9
```

Sometimes the digits in one of the places add to more than 9. Then you have to **regroup.** Regroup ones into tens and ones. Regroup tens into hundreds and tens.

Add: 247 + 485 = ☐

Regroup 12 ones into 1 ten and 2 ones.	Next, regroup 13 tens into 1 hundred and 3 tens.	Finally, add the hundreds.
$\overset{1}{}$ 247 +485 ───── 2	$\overset{11}{}$ 247 +485 ───── 32	$\overset{11}{}$ 247 +485 ───── 732

8   UNIT 1 Big Ideas from Grade 2

Think About It

If you add 99 to 99, will you have to regroup? Which places would you regroup and how would you regroup them?

_____

_____

PART 2 Focused Instruction

Use place-value blocks to model addition problems.

Add 45 and 16.

Draw place-value blocks to show 45.

Draw place-value blocks to show 16.

Combine the ones blocks. How many do you have? _____

Do you have to regroup the ones? _____

Show how you regroup the ones with place-value blocks.

Combine the tens blocks. Do not forget the ten that was regrouped. How many tens are there? _____

In the space above, draw the tens blocks.

What is 45 + 16? _____

UNIT 1 Big Ideas from Grade 2

Focused Instruction

Lesson 1

Add three-digit numbers the same way you add two-digit numbers. You may need to regroup.

Add 165 to 739.

Write this addition problem. Write one number under the other. Remember to keep the hundreds, tens, and ones lined up correctly.

How many ones are there? _____ Do you have to regroup? _____

In the space above, add the ones. Regroup if you have to.

In the space above, add the tens. Do you have to regroup? _____

In the space above, add the hundreds.

What is 165 + 739? _____

Use what you know about adding and regrouping to find these sums.

1 345 + 432 = _____

2 143 + 598 = _____

3 34 + 88 + 329 = _____

4 56 + 17 = _____

UNIT 1 Big Ideas from Grade 2

 **Guided Practice**   Lesson 1

Solve the following problems.

1 Model 18 + 9 with place-value blocks. Find the sum.

> Remember to regroup the ones.

Answer _____

2 A nature group plants 297 trees on Monday, 306 trees on Tuesday, and 288 trees on Wednesday.

Part A Write an addition sentence to show how many trees the group planted in all.

> You can add more than two numbers. You can add in any order.

Answer _____

Part B How many trees were planted by the end of Tuesday? Show your work.

Answer _____ trees

Part C Complete the addition to show how many trees were planted in all. Show your work.

Answer _____ trees

UNIT 1 Big Ideas from Grade 2

Part 4 Independent Practice — Lesson 1

Solve the following problems.

1 Add.   487
            +376

   A 863

   B 763

   C 853

   D 953

2 Look at this addition problem.

   586
   +219

   Part A Describe how the ones should be regrouped when adding.

   _____

   Part B Describe how the tens should be regrouped.

   _____

   Part C What is the sum?

   Answer _____

3 Colleen added 189 to 223.

   189
   +223
   402

   Describe the mistake that Colleen made.

   _____

   _____

Independent Practice — Lesson 1

4 Boris used place-value blocks to model an addition problem.

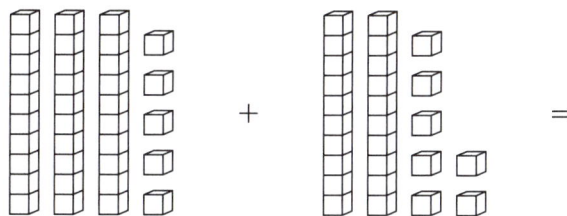

Part A Write the problem as an addition sentence.

_____

Part B Show the answer as a number by drawing place-value blocks.

5 Third-grade students at Riverview School are in two rooms, 401 and 402. The table shows how many boys and how many girls are in each room.

THIRD-GRADE STUDENTS AT RIVERVIEW SCHOOL

Room	Girls	Boys
401	14	19
402	17	15

Use the numbers in the table above to complete the table below.

THIRD-GRADE STUDENTS AT RIVERVIEW SCHOOL

Number of Girls	
Number of Boys	
Total Number of Third-Grade Students	

Independent Practice

6 In 2014, the city of Denver was 156 years old. The city of Los Angeles is 77 years older than Denver. The city of Boston is 151 years older than Los Angeles.

Part A How old was the city of Los Angeles in 2014? Show your work.

Answer _____ years

Part B How old was the city of Boston in 2014? Show your work.

Answer _____ years

LESSON 2: Subtracting Two- and Three-Digit Numbers

CCLS: 2.NBT.5, 7

Part 1 Introduction

Subtract means to take away. The answer to a subtraction problem is called the **difference**.

$5 - 3 = 2$
↑
Difference

Subtract the digits in the same place. Start with the ones place. Then subtract the numbers in the tens place, and then the hundreds place.

What is $47 - 23$?

Use place-value blocks to show 47.

First, subtract the ones.

```
  47
 -23
 ———
   4
```

Then subtract the tens.

```
  47
 -23
 ———
  24
```

Addition and subtraction are **inverse operations**. That means they are opposites. Use addition to check subtraction.

The place-value blocks that are left show that $47 - 23 = 24$.

Sometimes you must **regroup**. To regroup, change a ten into 10 ones. You can also change a hundred into 10 tens.

What is $247 - 63$?

Subtract the ones.

Subtract the tens. You cannot subtract 6 tens from 4 tens. You must regroup. Regroup 2 hundreds as 1 hundred and 10 tens.

```
  247
 - 63
 ————
    4
```

UNIT 1 Big Ideas from Grade 2

There is 1 hundred left in the hundreds place.
Add the regrouped tens to the tens you have:
  10 tens + 4 tens = 14 tens
There are 14 tens in the tens place.
Now you can subtract the tens.

```
  1 14
  2̷4̷7
 -  63
     84
```

Subtract the hundreds.

```
  1 14
  2̷4̷7
 -  63
    184
```

So 247 − 63 = 184.

Think About It

Choose two two-digit numbers and subtract the smaller number from the larger. How do you know if you must regroup?

_____

_____

PART 2 Focused Instruction

In Part 1, you learned that you can model numbers using place-value blocks. Use place-value blocks to find the answer to this subtraction problem.

Subtract 34 from 52.

Use this chart. Draw place-value blocks to show 52 in the first row. Draw place-value blocks to show 34 in the second row.

	Tens	Ones
52 =		
34 =		

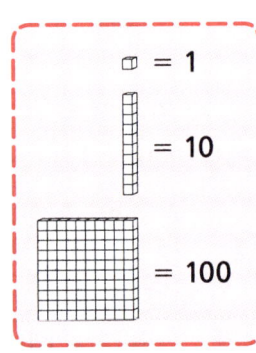

Focused Instruction — Lesson 2

How many ones blocks are in 52? _____

How many ones blocks are in 34? _____

Can you subtract 4 from 2? _____

How can you regroup the tens in 52? _____

Cross out a tens block and draw 10 ones blocks to show the regrouping.

Now subtract the ones. Cross out the ones blocks that are subtracted.

How many are left? _____

Now subtract the tens. Cross out the tens blocks that are subtracted.

How many are left? _____

What is 52 minus 34? _____

Count the remaining blocks to check your answer.

You cannot subtract from 0. You cannot regroup 0. Go to the next place and regroup.

Subtract:

$$605 - 47 = \underline{\hspace{2cm}}$$

605 has three digits, but 46 only has two. Be careful when lining up the digits.

What goes under the 5? _____

What goes under the 0? _____

Is there a number under the 6? _____

Write this subtraction problem with the larger number on top.

UNIT 1 Big Ideas from Grade 2

 **Focused Instruction** Lesson 2

You cannot subtract 7 from 5. You cannot regroup 0. You have to start by regrouping the 6 in the hundreds place. How do you regroup 6 hundreds?

_____

Now, regroup the 10 tens to get the ones you need.

How do you regroup the tens? _____

How many ones do you have now? _____

Now, you can subtract all three places.

What is the subtraction in the ones place? _____

What is the subtraction in the tens place? _____

What is the subtraction in the hundreds place? _____

What is 605 − 47? _____

Use what you know about subtracting to find these differences.

1 887 − 76 = _____

2 523 − 181 = _____

3 701 − 222 = _____

 **Guided Practice** — Lesson 2

Solve the following problems.

1. How much greater is 782 than 383? Show your work.

   All places will have to be regrouped. One place will have to be regrouped twice.

   Answer _____

2. Mara had a bag with 205 marbles in it. The bag broke, spilling the marbles. Some of the marbles were lost in the grass, but Mara was able to pick up 176 marbles.

   Part A How many marbles did Mara lose in the grass? Show your work.

   To subtract the ones, you will have to first regroup the hundreds and then the tens.

   Answer _____ marbles

   Part B Now use addition to check your answer. Show your work.

   Add your answer to the number you subtracted. The sum should be the number you subtracted from.

Part 4 Independent Practice — Lesson 2

Solve the following problems.

1. Subtract: 635
              −326

   A 209
   B 309
   C 311
   D 319

2. Subtract. Show your work.

   504 − 126 =

   Answer _____

3. Check True or False for each subtraction problem.

	True	False
101 − 99 = 12	☐	☐
746 − 643 = 103	☐	☐
462 − 253 = 219	☐	☐
301 − 108 = 193	☐	☐
500 − 111 = 389	☐	☐

Independent Practice

Lesson 2

4 When Denise woke up, the temperature was 49°F. At noon, the temperature had risen to 70°F. How many degrees did the temperature rise? Show your work.

Answer _____ °F

5 Karl is 24 years younger than his father. How old will Karl be when his father is 53? Show your work.

Answer _____ years old

6 Hideo's father raises sheep. He had 924 sheep. Then he sold 235 sheep to another farmer.

Part A How many sheep does Hideo's father have left? Show your work.

Answer _____ sheep

Part B Explain how you can use addition to check your answer to Part A.

_____
_____
_____

UNIT 1 Big Ideas from Grade 2

7 Sunnyvale Elementary School has 63 students in two third-grade classes. The class in room 201 has 34 students. The class in room 202 went on a field trip. If 15 boys went on the field trip, how many girls went on the field trip? Show your work.

Answer _____ girls

LESSON 3: Measuring Length

CCLS: 2.MD.1

Part 1 Introduction

Length is a measure of how long something is. You can measure a short length, such as your finger. You can also measure a long length, such as a football field.

A unit is a measure of length that stays the same. Each unit is always the same length no matter where or how you measure it. Common units of length are **inches (in.), feet (ft),** and **yards (yd).** These units are part of the **customary system** of measurement.

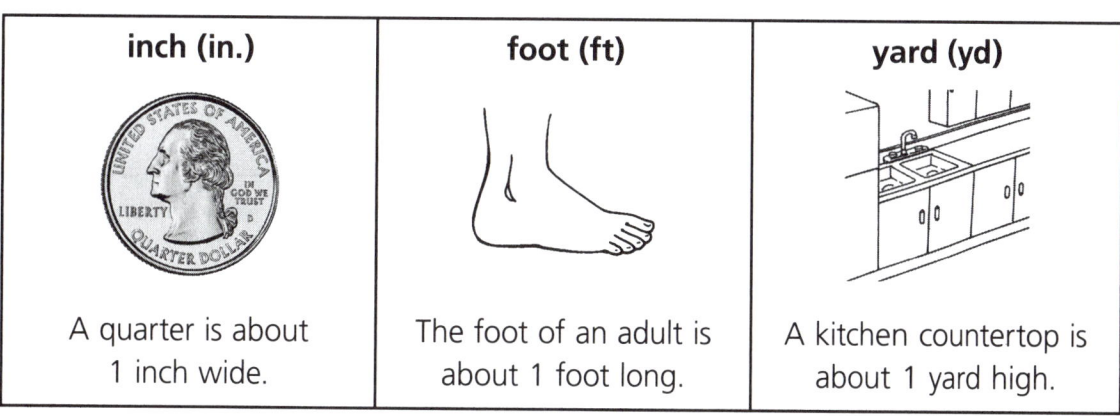

inch (in.)	foot (ft)	yard (yd)
A quarter is about 1 inch wide.	The foot of an adult is about 1 foot long.	A kitchen countertop is about 1 yard high.

Another system of measurement is the **metric system.** Units of length in this system are **meters (m)** and **centimeters (cm).** A meter is a little longer than a yard. There are 100 centimeters in one meter.

You can use different tools to measure length. A **ruler** is a tool used to measure short lengths. Line up the end of the object you are measuring with the zero-end of the ruler. Then read the measurement closest to the other end of the object.

This pencil is exactly 3 inches long.

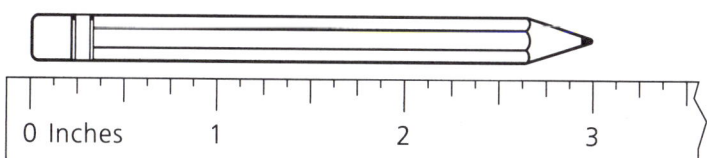

> Longer lengths are measured with yardsticks, meter sticks, and measuring tapes.

UNIT 1 Big Ideas from Grade 2

Measuring is easier if we choose long tools to measure long lengths and short tools to measure short lengths. Also, it is best to choose small units to measure small things and large units to measure large things. For example:

- Use inches or centimeters to measure the length of a pencil.
- Use feet to measure the width of a bedroom.
- Use yards or meters to measure the length of a soccer field.

Think About It

Sarah wants to measure the length of her cat's whiskers. Which would be the best measuring tool to use? Which units should she use for her results? Explain your choices.

_____
_____
_____

PART 2 Focused Instruction

Choose an appropriate measuring tool. Choose the best units to use to measure short or long objects.

Measure the length of the spoon in metric units.

Is the spoon short or long compared to a meter stick?

_____

Which tool is used to measure short things? _____

How do you measure something with a measuring tool?

_____
_____

> Use the measuring tools that you have.

 **Focused Instruction** Lesson 3

Which units are good for measuring short things? _____

How long is the spoon? _____

With a partner, choose a measuring tool or tools to measure the width of your classroom. You can choose from rulers, yardsticks, meter sticks, and measuring tapes.

Which measuring tools are best for measuring the width of your classroom?
_____

Which customary units would be best to use?
_____

Which metric units would be best to use?
_____

How wide is your classroom? _____

Compare your results with those of other pairs of students. Discuss reasons for any differences.

Use what you know about measuring to answer these questions.

1 Which tool would you use to measure your height in customary units?
_____

2 Which metric unit would you use to measure the length of a carrot?
_____

3 What is the length of your thumb in inches and in centimeters?
_____

Guided Practice

Lesson 3

Solve the following problems.

1 Think about measurement tools.

> Remember the tool should be close to the size of the object being measured.

Part A Which tool would be best to measure the length of a rabbit's ear? Explain why this is the best tool.

_____

_____

Part B Which tool would be best to measure the width of a house? Explain why this is the best tool.

_____

_____

2 What is the length of this feather in inches?

> Remember how to place the ruler and the object you are measuring.

Answer _____ inches

Independent Practice

Lesson 3

Solve the following problems.

1. Which of these objects would be easy to measure with a measuring tape, but hard to measure with a ruler? Select the **three** correct answers.

   A the width of a door

   B the width of your finger

   C the height of a table

   D the depth of a teacup

   E the height of a ladder

2. What is the length, in centimeters, of this grasshopper? Measure to the tip of the antennae.

   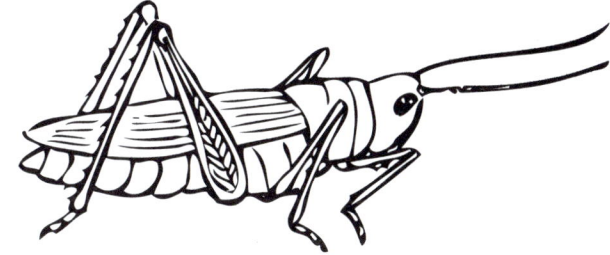

   Answer _____ centimeters

3. Brandon has a snack bag that is 5 inches long. He wants to put some pretzel rods like the one below in the bag. He wants the pretzel rods to lie flat in the bag. Will this pretzel rod fit in Brandon's bag? Explain your answer.

   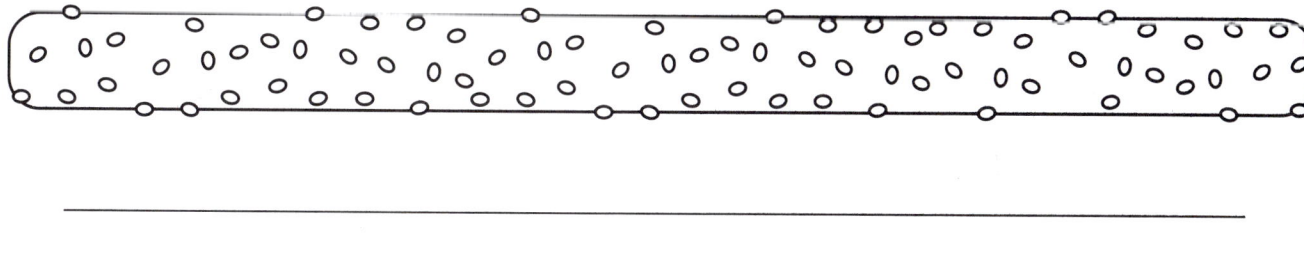

   _____

   _____

UNIT 1 Big Ideas from Grade 2

Independent Practice — Lesson 3

4 Use your inch ruler to draw a line that is 2 inches long.

5 Measure the block of wood with your centimeter ruler. Will the block of wood fit through the hole in the board? Explain your answer.

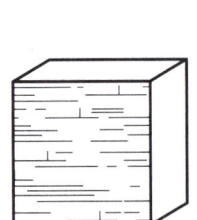
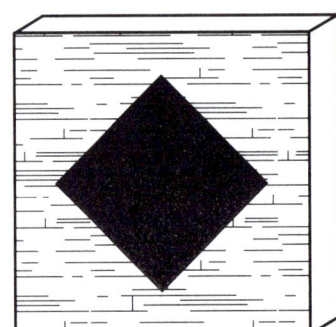

_____
_____

6 Kim wants to give this toy car to her brother as a gift. She wants to make a box to put it in before she wraps the gift.

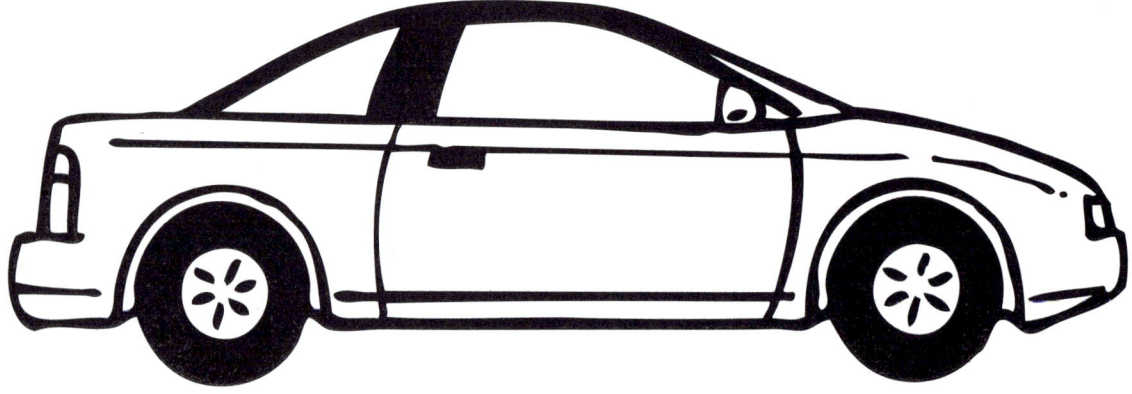

How long does the box need to be? How high does it need to be?

Length _____ inches

Height _____ inches

28 UNIT 1 Big Ideas from Grade 2

Lesson 4: Tiling Rectangles

CCLS: 2.G.2

Part 1 Introduction

Flat shapes are called **plane figures.** The amount of space inside a plane figure is called its **area.** You can divide a plane figure into same-size squares and count the total number of them.

The length of each side of this square is 1 inch. The area of the square is 1 square inch. How many of these squares can fit in this rectangle?

> Any square is a square unit.
>
> A square that has 1-centimeter sides is 1 square centimeter. A square that has 1-foot sides is 1 square foot.

Make rows of squares. Each row has the same number of squares. Count the squares. There are 2 rows of 3 squares. There are 6 squares in all. The space inside the rectangle is 6 square inches. So the area of the rectangle is 6 square inches. Dividing a rectangle into equal squares like this is called **tiling.**

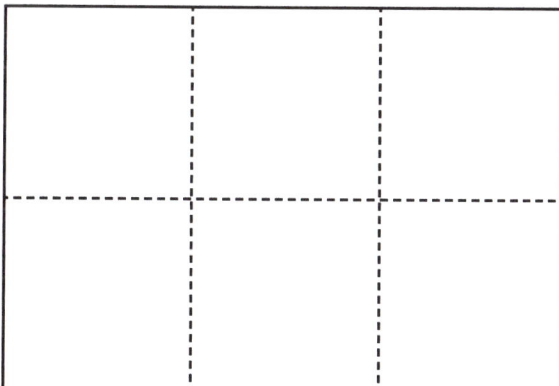

Think About It

Think of something in real life that is shaped like a rectangle. When might you need to use tiling?

_____
_____

PART 2 Focused Instruction

Use tiling to find the area of rectangles. Be sure that each square is the same size. The squares should cover the entire rectangle.

This rectangle is divided into equal squares. What is the area of the rectangle?

What can be used as a unit in this problem? _____

If one square equals one square unit, how do you find the area of the whole rectangle? _____

What is the area of the rectangle? _____

Use tiling to find areas of common objects. Work with a partner to find the area of rectangles in your classroom. Use your counters. Each counter is 1 square inch.

What is the area of the cover of your math book? _____

What is the area of the top of your desk? _____

Tell how you can use the squares to find an area.

_____
_____

Focused Instruction Lesson 4

Use what you know about rectangles, area, and tiling to answer these questions.

1. How many squares like the one below can you fit in this rectangle? Use your inch ruler to help you.

   _____

2. What is the area of this rectangle?

   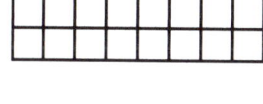

   _____

UNIT 1 Big Ideas from Grade 2

Guided Practice

Lesson 4

Solve the following problems.

1 These rectangles are made up of squares that are the same size.

> A larger rectangle can fit more squares inside it.

Order the rectangles from smallest to largest according to the number of squares.

Answer _____

2 Latifa's bedroom is not a rectangle. It is shaped like the figure below.

Part A Show how you can divide Latifa's room into two rectangles by drawing a line.

Part B Use this square  as a square unit to find the area of each rectangle. What are the areas of the rectangles?

Answer _____ and _____ square units

Part C What is the area of Latifa's whole room?

> Add the areas of the two rectangles to get the total area of the room.

Answer _____ square units

Independent Practice

Solve the following problems.

1. Look at the rectangle and the square.

   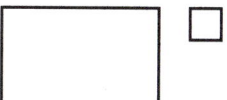

   Tile the rectangle into squares that are the size of the small square.

   Part A How many rows can you make?

   Answer _____ rows

   Part B How many squares are in each row?

   Answer _____ squares

2. This rectangle is twice as long as it is wide.

   Part A How many squares are in this rectangle?

   Answer _____ squares

   Part B Hector made a rectangle with 6 rows of 3 squares. He says it is the same size as this rectangle. Is Hector correct? How do you know?

   _____

   _____

Independent Practice

Lesson 4

3 In the rectangles below, all the small squares are the same size.

Part A Which three of these rectangles have the same area? Select the **three** correct answers.

A

B

C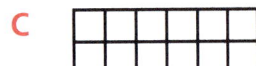

D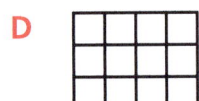

E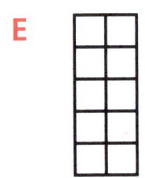

Part B Explain how you found the answer to Part A.

_____
_____
_____
_____

Independent Practice — Lesson 4

4 Which of these rectangles can be divided into four equal squares? Check Yes or No.

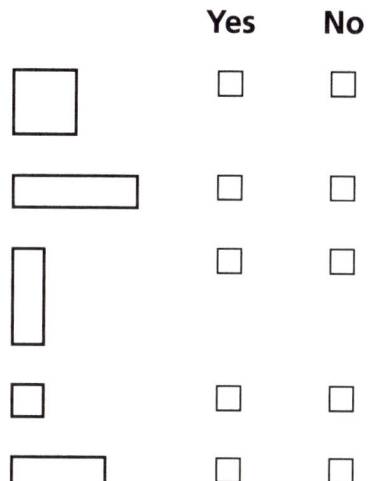

5 A worker is putting tiles on this bathroom floor. The tiles are squares that are the same size.

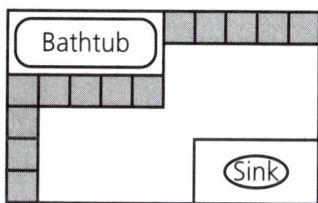

So far, the worker has laid down the tiles shown. He has 30 tiles left to finish the job. Will that be enough?

Answer _____

Explain how you found out how many tiles the worker needs to finish.

_____

_____

_____

Independent Practice — Lesson 4

6 Amaya is making a small square patio in her backyard. She is using square stones that measure 1 foot on each side.

Part A What unit is each stone?

Answer _____

Part B Amaya covers an area with the stones as shown below.

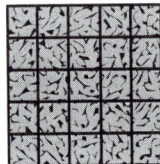

What is the area of Amaya's patio?

Answer _____ square feet

CCLS: 2.G.1

Flat shapes are called **plane figures.** A plane figure is a **polygon** if its sides meet and it does not have any openings. The sides of a polygon meet to form a corner, called an **angle.** The number of angles in a polygon is the same as the number of sides. A **regular polygon** has angles that are the same size and sides that are the same length. The table shows four kinds of polygons.

POLYGONS

Shape	Name	Number of Sides	Number of Angles
△	Triangle	3	3
▭	Quadrilateral	4	4
⬠	Pentagon	5	5
⬡	Hexagon	6	6

Each type of polygon can have many different forms. For example, all of the figures below are triangles because they have three sides and three angles.

All quadrilaterals have four sides and four angles, but they can be very different. These are all quadrilaterals.

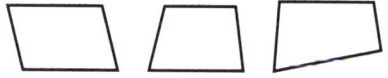

A **rectangle** is a type of quadrilateral. It has opposite sides that are the same length. It has four square corners. A **square** is a type of rectangle with sides that are all the same length.

Rectangle   Square

UNIT 1 Big Ideas from Grade 2

Think About It

Describe two polygons around you right now. How are they the same? How are they different?

_____

_____

PART 2 Focused Instruction

You can identify polygons by the number of sides and angles. Work with a partner as you name these polygons.

Look at this group of polygons.

[Figures: 1 rectangle, 2 pentagon, 3 quadrilateral, 4 parallelogram, 5 triangle, 6 triangle]

Find the quadrilaterals.

How many sides does a quadrilateral have? _____

Does the size of the sides and angles tell you whether or not a figure is a quadrilateral? _____

Which figures are quadrilaterals? _____

> How are rectangles different from other quadrilaterals? Remember that squares are a type of rectangle.

Find the rectangles.

Are all angles of a rectangle the same? _____

Which figures are rectangles? _____

Find the polygons that are not quadrilaterals.

How many sides do triangles have? _____ Pentagons? _____

Hexagons? _____

Is there a triangle? If so, which is it? _____

Is there a pentagon? If so, which is it? _____

Is there a hexagon? If so, which is it? _____

38 UNIT 1 Big Ideas from Grade 2

Focused Instruction — Lesson 5

Use a ruler to draw polygons. With a partner, look for different polygons in your classroom.

Draw a picture of a triangle you found.

How do you know it is a triangle?
_____

Draw a picture of a quadrilateral you found.

How do you know it is a quadrilateral?
_____

Describe another polygon in the classroom. What is its name?
_____

Draw the polygon.

Use what you know about polygons to answer these questions.

1 Name the figure at the right.
   _____

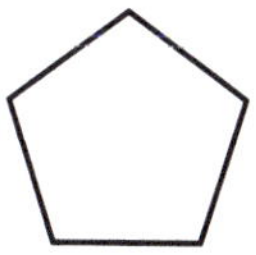

2 A figure has 3 sides and 3 angles. What is the name of the figure?
   _____

Part 3 Guided Practice — Lesson 5

Solve the following problems.

1. In baseball, a batter stands at home plate and tries to hit the ball. Home plate is a flat piece of rubber with this shape.

   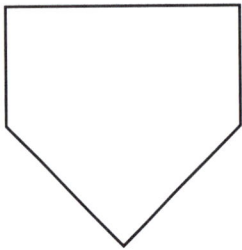

   What polygon is home plate?

   Answer _____

   Count the sides.

2. Carmen made a birthday card for her friend. It has 4 sides and 4 angles. Opposite sides of the card are the same length. The corners are square.

   Part A Draw the birthday card in the space below.

   Part B What kind of polygon is the birthday card?

   Answer _____

   Squares and rectangles both have square corners. How are they different?

Independent Practice

Lesson 5

Solve the following problems.

1 A polygon has four sides. The sides are 3 inches, 4 inches, 5 inches, and 6 inches. What is the name of this polygon?

A square

B triangle

C quadrilateral

D rectangle

2 Isaac's grandmother made a quilt for his bed. She sewed small pieces of cloth together as shown. She used two colors of cloth that were all the same shape.

Part A Name the polygon she used for the cloth pieces. Explain how you know.

_____

_____

Part B Isaac's grandmother sewed together two of the pieces of cloth. What is one kind of shape that the two pieces make when put together? Explain.

_____

_____

UNIT 1 Big Ideas from Grade 2

Independent Practice

Lesson 5

3 Complete the table.

Figure	Number of Sides	Number of Angles	Name
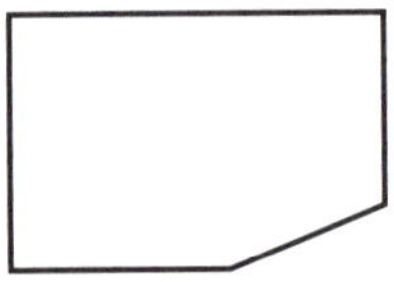			
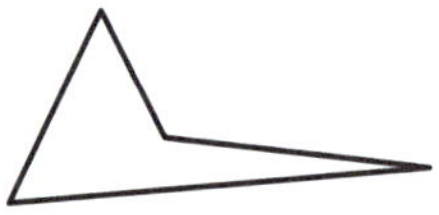			
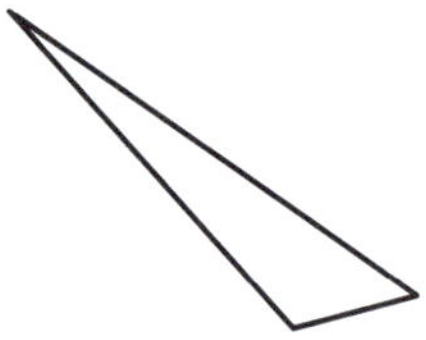			

4 The table lists polygons in the first column. Put a check in each box that describes that figure. Check all the boxes that are true for each polygon.

Polygon	Square	Rectangle	Quadrilateral

UNIT 1 Big Ideas from Grade 2

Independent Practice Lesson 5

5 Draw the polygon described in each box.

| Draw a regular hexagon. |

| Draw a pentagon that is not regular. |

6 Look at the pattern shown here.

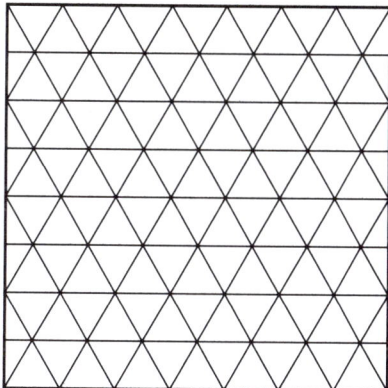

Find these four polygons in the pattern. Find one of each. Draw heavy lines to show each of the polygons. Write the correct letter inside each shape to show which it is.

  A   a triangle with three equal sides

  B   a quadrilateral that is not a rectangle

  C   a regular hexagon

  D   a hexagon that is not regular

UNIT 1 Big Ideas from Grade 2

UNIT 1 REVIEW
Big Ideas from Grade 2

CCLS: 2.NBT.5, 7; 2.MD.1; 2.G.1, 2

Solve the following problems.

1. What is the sum of 215 and 177? Show your work.

   Answer _____

2. Would you use a centimeter ruler or a meter stick to measure the length of a cat's ear? Explain your answer.

   _____
   _____

3. A farmer pulled 127 carrots and 91 beets out of the ground. How many vegetables did the farmer pull out of the ground in all? Show your work.

   Answer _____ vegetables

4 Use the centimeter side of your ruler to measure these objects.

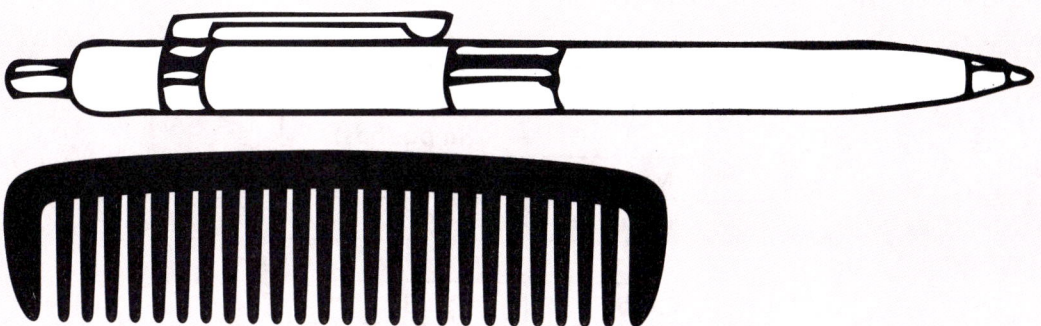

Part A How long is the pen?

Answer _____ centimeters

Part B How long is the comb?

Answer _____ centimeters

5 President George Washington was born in the year 1732. President Abraham Lincoln was born in 1809.

Part A How many years passed from the birth of Washington to the birth of Lincoln? Show your work.

Answer _____ years

Part B Use an addition sentence to check your answer.

Answer _____

6 Four people on a fishing trip each caught one fish. The table shows the weights of the fish they caught.

WEIGHT OF FISH

Name of Person	Weight of Fish (in pounds)
Min	13
Julio	23
Erin	18
Carlo	32

Part A What was the difference between the weight of the heaviest fish and the weight of the lightest fish? Show your work.

Answer _____ pounds

Part B Erin and Min weigh their fish together. They think the weight of their fish together is more than the weight of Carlo's fish. Are Erin and Min correct? Show how you know.

_____

_____

7 Measure the length, in centimeters, of one side of each shape. In each shape, all the sides are the same length. Name the two shapes that have sides that are equal to each other.

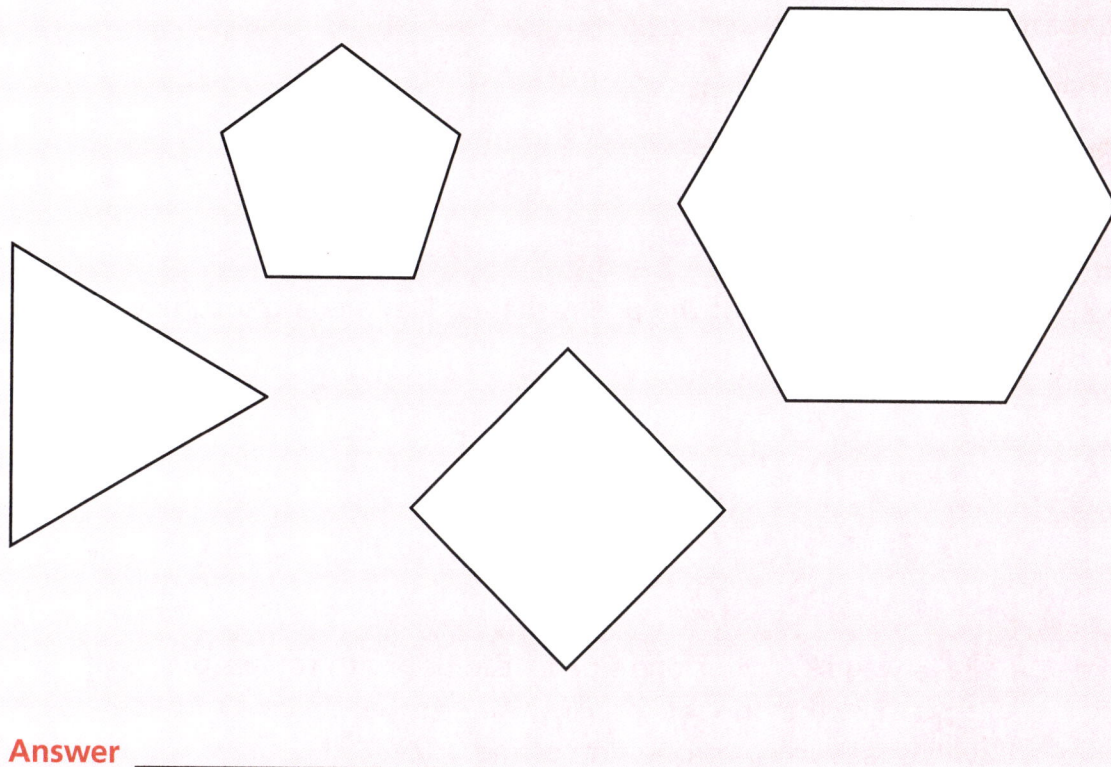

Answer _____

8 The rectangle below is made up of squares that are the same size.

Draw two different rectangles that have the same number of squares as the one above. Show the squares. Do not draw a rectangle with only one row of squares.

9 How many corners does each of these shapes have?

Pentagon _____ corners

Square _____ corners

Triangle _____ corners

Rectangle _____ corners

Hexagon _____ corners

10 Laila has a box. Each side of the box is shaped like the larger square below.

Paper

Part A Laila wants to cover one side of the box with square pieces of paper like the one shown. How many square pieces of paper will it take to cover one side of the box?

Answer _____ pieces of paper

Part B Show how the square pieces of paper fit on this side of the box.

Part C How many square pieces of paper would it take to cover all 6 sides of the box? Explain your answer.

_____

_____

11 Think about different quadrilaterals.

   Part A Draw a quadrilateral that is **not** a square and **not** a rectangle.

   Part B Draw a quadrilateral that is a rectangle but **not** a square.

   Part C Draw a quadrilateral that is a rectangle with 4 equal sides.

   Part D Draw a quadrilateral that has 4 equal sides and is neither a square nor a rectangle.

12 The figure below is a combination of different shapes. Look for groups of lines that form different plane figures.

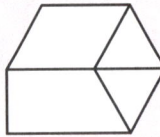

Part A Color one of the triangles in the figure.

Part B Find three quadrilaterals. Draw each one in the space below.

Part C Find one hexagon that is **not** a regular hexagon. Draw the hexagon in the space below.

13 The blocks are a model of a number.

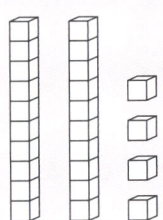

Part A What number do these blocks show?

Answer _____

Part B Subtract 13 from the number above. Cross out the blocks to show the number you subtracted.

Part C What number does the model show now?

Answer _____

UNIT 2
Operations and Algebraic Thinking, Part 1

In grade 2, you learned how to add and subtract numbers and use arrays. Now you can use what you know about addition and subtraction to multiply, divide, and find patterns using numbers.

LESSON 6 Understanding Multiplication In this lesson, you will use repeated addition and multiplication sentences to solve problems.

LESSON 7 Properties of Multiplication In this lesson, you will use the commutative, associative, and distributive properties to solve problems.

LESSON 8 Understanding Division In this lesson, you will learn that division involves splitting numbers into even groups and will solve different problems by dividing.

LESSON 9 Connecting Multiplication and Division In this lesson, you will use unknown factors to help you understand inverse operations and solve division problems.

LESSON 10 Multiplication Facts In this lesson, you will practice working with the different operation properties and understanding inverse operations when solving multiplication problems.

LESSON 11 Division Facts In this lesson, you will practice working with the different operation properties and understanding inverse operations when solving division problems.

LESSON 12 Patterns In this lesson, you will use skip counting, addition, and multiplication tables to find patterns among numbers.

Lesson 6: Understanding Multiplication

CCLS: 3.OA.1

Part 1 Introduction

Multiply to put together groups of the same size.

Bethany spills the pennies from her piggy bank. How can she use multiplication to count them?

Bethany can arrange the pennies in an **array.** An array has rows with the same number of objects. Bethany has 3 rows of 5 pennies.

Bethany can add 5 pennies 3 times to find the total. This is called **repeated addition.**

$$5 + 5 + 5 = 15$$

52 UNIT 2 Operations and Algebraic Thinking, Part 1

Bethany can also multiply.

$$3 \times 5 = 15$$

Number of groups   Number in each group

Factors are the numbers being multiplied. The answer is the **product**.

Think About It

Eduardo baked rolls for a family party. Each pan had 6 rows of rolls. There were 4 rolls in each row. Explain how the rolls are like an array. How can Eduardo find how many rolls he made?

_____

_____

_____

PART 2 Focused Instruction

Multiplication problems can be described using an array. The number of rows is one factor. The number of shapes in each row is another factor. The total number of shapes is the product.

★ ★ ★ ★ ★ ★ ★
★ ★ ★ ★ ★ ★ ★
★ ★ ★ ★ ★ ★ ★
★ ★ ★ ★ ★ ★ ★
★ ★ ★ ★ ★ ★ ★
★ ★ ★ ★ ★ ★ ★
★ ★ ★ ★ ★ ★ ★
★ ★ ★ ★ ★ ★ ★
★ ★ ★ ★ ★ ★ ★

> Think of each row as a group.

How many groups are there? _____

How many stars are in each group? _____

What number do you add repeatedly? _____

How many times do you add it? _____

Write the multiplication sentence. _____

Focused Instruction — Lesson 6

Think about what the numbers in a word problem mean. Solve this problem using a multiplication sentence.

Carla picked peaches and put them in a basket. She carried 4 peaches at a time. She stopped when the basket was full. It took her 8 trips to fill the basket. How many peaches did Carla pick?

What are the parts of a multiplication sentence?
_____

How many factors are in the multiplication sentence that solves this problem?
_____

> A factor is a number being multiplied.

Describe one of the factors.
_____

Describe the other factor. _____

Solve the problem using a multiplication sentence. _____

Use what you know about multiplication to write multiplication sentences to answer these questions.

1. A group of friends went to a picnic in 4 cars. Each car had 5 people in it. How many people went to the picnic?

   _____

2. Tricycles have 3 wheels. How many wheels do 7 tricycles have?

   _____

3. A room has 6 rows of chairs. Each row has 9 chairs. How many chairs are in the room?

   _____

Guided Practice

Lesson 6

Solve the following problems.

1. Write a multiplication sentence that goes with the array below.

> One factor is the number of rows. The other factor is the number of objects in each row.

Answer _____

2. Draw an array that models the multiplication sentence:

    $2 \times 5 = 10$

> In a multiplication sentence, the number of groups is written first. In an array, each row is a group.

3. Write an addition sentence and related multiplication sentence that represent the drawing below.

> Remember how addition sentences are related to multiplication sentences.

Addition _____

Multiplication _____

UNIT 2 Operations and Algebraic Thinking, Part 1

Part 4 Independent Practice — Lesson 6

Solve the following problems.

1 Which array models 3 × 2 = 6?

A (2 × 2 array)

B (3 × 2 array)

C (2 × 4 array)

D (3 × 2 array)

2 Each of the 4 wheels of a car is held on by 5 bolts. Which multiplication sentence shows the total number of wheel bolts on a car?

A 4 × 4 = 20

B 5 × 5 = 20

C 4 × 5 = 20

D 4 × 4 × 4 × 4 × 4 = 20

3 Can you write 6 + 6 + 6 + 4 = 22 as a multiplication sentence? Explain.

_____

_____

UNIT 2 Operations and Algebraic Thinking, Part 1

Independent Practice — Lesson 6

4 Emilio planted 4 rows of tomato plants. Each row had 6 plants.

Part A Write the multiplication sentence that shows how many tomato plants Emilio planted. Solve the problem.

Answer _____

Part B Draw the array that shows the multiplication sentence.

Part C Draw an array to show another way that Emilio could have arranged the same number of tomato plants other than in a single row.

5 Look at the drawing at the right. Rama wrote the addition sentence and the multiplication sentence below to put together the equal groups. Is she correct? Explain.

$$5 + 5 + 5 + 5 + 5 = 25$$
$$5 \times 5 = 25$$

_____
_____
_____

UNIT 2 Operations and Algebraic Thinking, Part 1

Independent Practice

Lesson 6

6 George and Elsa put trays of cookies in the oven to bake. George made 3 rows of cookies with 4 cookies in each row. Elsa made 4 rows of cookies with 3 cookies in each row.

Part A In the space below, draw an array to show how George placed the cookies. Then draw an array to show how Elsa placed the cookies.

Part B Write a multiplication sentence for each array. Then select an option to complete the sentence below.

George's Array _____

Elsa's Array _____

The number of cookies George made was [less than, more than, the same as] the number of cookies Elsa made.

Properties of Multiplication

CCLS: 3.OA.5

Part 1 Introduction

When you multiply, you can change the order of the factors. The product will stay the same. This is known as the **commutative property.**

Ian has 6 baseball cards. He wants to arrange them in an album. He can make 2 rows of 3 cards. He can also make 3 rows of 2 cards.

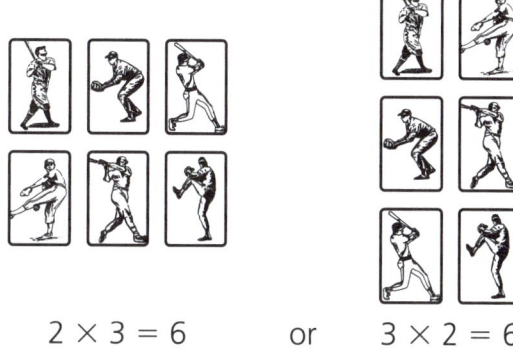

2 × 3 = 6   or   3 × 2 = 6

Sometimes you need to multiply more than two numbers. The **associative property** tells you that you can multiply in any order and the product will be the same. Parentheses, ( ), show which numbers to multiply first.

$$(2 \times 4) \times 5 \qquad\qquad 2 \times (4 \times 5)$$
$$8 \times 5 \qquad\qquad 2 \times 20$$
$$40 \leftarrow \text{The product is the same.} \rightarrow 40$$

> The commutative and associative properties are also true for addition. They are **not** true for division or subtraction.

Sometimes it is helpful to break apart a number before you multiply. The **distributive property** lets you multiply a number by a sum.

To multiply 5 × 14, break 14 into smaller numbers to make multiplying easier.

Find two numbers that add to 14: 10 + 4.

Then rewrite the multiplication: 5 × (10 + 4).

Multiply each addend by 5: 5 × 10 = 50 and 5 × 4 = 20.

Add the products: 50 + 20 = 70, so 5 × 14 = 70.

UNIT 2 Operations and Algebraic Thinking, Part 1

Think About It

The distributive property gives you choices. You can break apart a large number in several ways. Suppose you want to solve this multiplication sentence: 6 × 15. Breaking 15 into 2 + 13 does not make the math easier. What would be more helpful? What other numbers add up to 15? Which numbers would you use?

_____

_____

_____

PART 2 Focused Instruction

Use the commutative property to think about multiplication problems.

Joel is arranging 35 chairs in a classroom. He wants to have the same number of chairs in each row. First, he tries making 5 rows with 7 chairs in each row. He finds the room is too narrow to put 7 chairs in a row. Sonia says it would also work to make 7 rows of 5 chairs. Is Sonia right? Why or why not?

What are the two multiplication sentences for this problem?

_____

What does the commutative property tell you about these multiplication sentences?

_____

Does this show that Sonia is right? _____

You can use different properties to help you solve the same problem. Think about both the associative property and the distributive property as you answer the following questions.

Olivia's school has 3 small school buses. Each bus has 28 seats.

To find the total number of seats, you can think about the distributive property.

Focused Instruction

What does the distributive property allow you to do to a factor in a multiplication problem?

_____

_____

What two numbers can you add together to get 28? _____

Write and solve a multiplication problem to solve this problem.

_____

You can also use the associative property.

What does the associative property say about three factors?

_____

_____

What are two numbers that can be multiplied to get 28, other than 1 and 28?

_____

Write a multiplication problem with three factors using the two numbers you wrote above and the third factor from the problem.

_____

Solve your multiplication problem. _____

Are your answers to the two problems the same? _____

Which way do you think was the easier way to solve the problem?

_____

_____

Use what you know about the properties of multiplication to fill in the missing numbers in these problems.

1 $7 \times 3 = 3 \times$ _____

2 $(3 \times 4) \times 5 = 3 \times (4 \times$ _____ $)$

3 $9 \times 21 = 9 \times (10 +$ _____ $)$

Part 3 Guided Practice — Lesson 7

Solve the following problems.

1 These arrays show people watching a game from the stands. The stands are at different places by the field.

Side of the Field

End of the Field

> You usually write the number of rows first when writing a multiplication sentence for an array. Putting that number second does not change the product.

Part A Write multiplication sentences for each group.

Answer _____

Part B Which multiplication property does this problem show?

Answer _____

2 Look at the multiplication sentence.

$$(4 \times 8) \times 2 = 32 \times 2 = 64$$

Part A What do the parentheses show?

> What does the associative property say about multiplying more than two numbers?

Answer _____

Part B Write the multiplication sentence in a different way to show the associative property of multiplication.

Answer _____

3 How can the fact $3 \times 7 = 21$ help you find the product of 6×7?

_____
_____

> The distributive property shows you how to break apart a factor to make a multiplication problem easier.

UNIT 2 Operations and Algebraic Thinking, Part 1

PART 4 Independent Practice — Lesson 7

Solve the following problems.

1 What number is missing in the number sentence below?

$$4 \times (7 \times 3) = (\square \times 7) \times 3$$

A 3

B 4

C 7

D 21

2 Look at the unfinished multiplication sentence:

$$(5 \times 9) \times 8 = \square$$

There are several ways to finish the sentence. Which shows the associative property?

A $5 \times 9 \times (4 + 4)$

B $5 \times (9 \times 8)$

C $(9 \times 5) \times 8$

D 45×8

3 Which multiplication sentence shows the distributive property?

A $4 \times 2 \times 5 = 5 \times 2 \times 4$

B $4 \times (2 \times 5) = (4 \times 2) \times 5$

C $4 \times 10 = 4 \times (5 + 5)$

D $4 \times 2 \times 5 = 4 \times (2 + 5)$

UNIT 2 Operations and Algebraic Thinking, Part 1

Independent Practice — Lesson 7

4 Christine hiked in the forest at a speed of 3 miles per hour for 2 hours. She multiplied and found that she hiked 2 × 3 = 6 miles. On her way home, she was tired. So Christine's speed was only 2 miles per hour coming back. It took her 3 hours to hike back.

Part A Write a number sentence to show Christine's distance for her hike back.

Answer _____

Part B Which property of multiplication is used in this problem?

    A commutative

    B associative

    C distributive

Part C Explain your answer to Part B.

_____

_____

5 Which expression is the same as 16 × 6?

  A (8 × 6) + (2 × 6)

  B (3 + 6) + (7 × 6)

  C (9 × 6) + (7 × 6)

  D (4 × 6) + (4 × 6)

6 Explain how to find the product of 13 × 9 by using the distributive property.

_____

_____

Independent Practice — Lesson 7

7 Nina and Alejandro are working on math problems to review the properties of multiplication.

Part A Nina writes the multiplication sentence $2 \times 6 = 12$. Alejandro writes the multiplication sentence $3 \times 4 = 12$. Alejandro says the products are the same because of the commutative property of multiplication. Is he correct? Explain.

_____

_____

_____

_____

Part B Nina says that the product of $5 \times 4 \times 3$ is greater than the product of $3 \times 4 \times 5$. Is she correct? Explain.

_____

_____

_____

_____

Lesson 8: Understanding Division

Part 1 Introduction

Division is sharing a number of objects equally. When you divide, think of placing objects into groups so that each group has the same number of objects.

A pet shop owner got a delivery of 15 fish. She wants to divide them evenly among 3 fish tanks. How many fish should she put in each fish tank?

Place one fish at a time in each fish tank until you run out of fish. Then count the number of fish in each fish tank.

 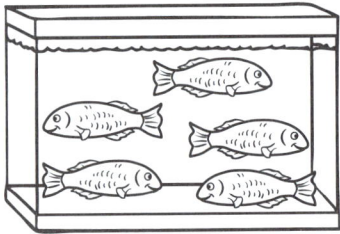 

There are 5 fish in each fish tank. The 15 fish can be divided into 3 groups of 5 fish.

Think of division as **repeated subtraction.** Keep subtracting until you reach 0.

$15 - 3 = 12$
$12 - 3 = 9$
$9 - 3 = 6$
$6 - 3 = 3$
$3 - 3 = 0$ You can subtract 3 five times. So $15 \div 3 = 5$.

You can show division with a number sentence. The number being divided is the **dividend.** The number doing the dividing is the **divisor.** The answer to a division problem is the **quotient.**

$$15 \div 3 = 5$$

Dividend: Total number of fish   Quotient: Number of fish in each tank

Divisor: Number of fish tanks

Think About It

Explain how you can use division when you are sharing stickers with some friends.

_____

_____

PART 2 Focused Instruction

Use pictures to help you divide. In division, you make groups of equal sizes.

Marco has 24 red roses. He wants to put an equal number of roses in 3 different vases. How many roses should Marco put in each vase?

What is the total number of roses? _____

How many groups will there be? _____

Draw circles around the roses to make 3 equal groups.

How many roses are in each group? _____

Write this problem as a division sentence. _____

Focused Instruction

Lesson 8

Think about what each part of the division problem tells you.

Simone wants to share a box of candy with some friends. She uses this equation to divide the pieces of candy into equal groups.

$$20 \div 5 = 4$$

How many pieces of candy are in the box? _____

How many groups does Simone want to make? _____

What might this number represent? _____

How many are in each group? _____

What might this number represent? _____

Use what you know about division to answer these questions.

1 There are 18 sheep. A farmer wants to put the same number of sheep on each of 3 different fields. How many sheep should the farmer put on each field?

_____

2 Myra has 24 pictures. She wants to put the same number of pictures on each page of her album. Her album has 6 pages. How many pictures should Myra put on each page?

_____

UNIT 2 Operations and Algebraic Thinking, Part 1

Guided Practice

Solve the following problems.

1 Mrs. Lopez takes her 3 children to the carnival. She has 12 quarters. She wants to give the same number of quarters to each child to play a game. How many quarters will each child get?

> Circle three groups of quarters. Find the number of quarters in each group.

Answer _____ quarters

2 A farmer collects 72 eggs from his hens. He puts them in egg cartons that each hold 12 eggs. How many cartons of eggs can the farmer fill? Show your work using repeated subtraction.

> Remember to subtract the number of eggs in each group.

Answer _____ cartons

3 Janice uses beads to make bracelets. She uses the number sentence shown to separate her beads.

$$36 \div 9 = 4$$

Write a statement that describes this number sentence.

> The statement should include each number in the number sentence.

_____

_____

Independent Practice

Lesson 8

Solve the following problems.

1 Which equation best represents the picture?

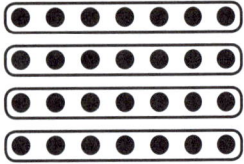

A 7 × 1 = 7

B 28 ÷ 4 = 7

C 28 − 7 = 21

D 7 ÷ 7 = 1

2 Nick has 42 sticks of gum. He says that he can share the sticks equally among 5 people. Is he correct? Explain. Draw a model to help explain your answer.

_____

_____

_____

3 Students sit at tables in art club. Each table has 7 chairs. There are 56 students in art club. Students can fill each table without any students or chairs left over.

56 ÷ 7 = 8

What does the quotient, 8, represent in this problem?

A the number of students at each table

B the number of chairs in the room

C the number of tables needed

D the number of chairs that are empty

Independent Practice — Lesson 8

4 Gia buys 20 plants. She wants to put 4 plants together in a pot. Which number sentence shows the number of pots that Gia needs?

   A $20 + 4 = 24$

   B $20 \div 4 = 5$

   C $20 - 4 = 16$

   D $5 \times 4 = 20$

5 Leo and his father are building a birdhouse for their backyard.

Part A Leo and his father buy a wooden rod that is 54 inches long. They need to make 10 shorter rods. Each rod must be 6 inches long. Do they have enough wood to make all 10 pieces? Explain your answer using division.

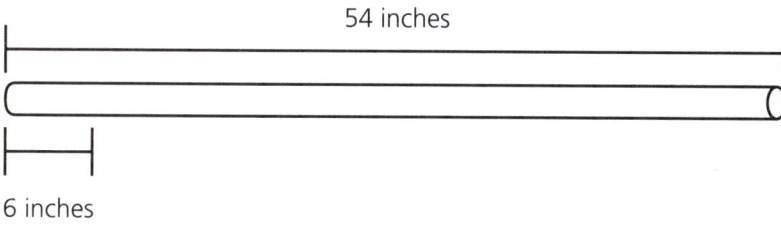

_____
_____
_____

Part B Leo says that he and his father should have bought a 60-inch rod to get 10 pieces that are 6 inches long. Is he correct? Explain.

_____
_____
_____

Independent Practice — Lesson 8

6 The 18 dots in the model represent students who play sports at a school.

Part A The softball coach wants to show that the 18 players can be divided into 2 teams.

$$18 \div 2 = 9$$

How can the coach draw groups to show this problem? Explain what the 9 represents.

_____

_____

Part B The soccer coach wants to show that the 18 players can be divided into teams of 3 players.

$$18 \div 3 = 6$$

How can the coach draw groups to show this problem? Explain what the 6 represents.

_____

_____

CCLS: 3.OA.6

Lesson 9: Connecting Multiplication and Division

Part 1: Introduction

Multiplication and division are **inverse operations.** This means that they are opposites. One operation undoes the other.

$$2 \times 3 = 6 \text{ and } 6 \div 3 = 2$$
$$3 \times 2 = 6 \text{ and } 6 \div 2 = 3$$

The numbers 2, 3, and 6 make up a **fact family.** The diagrams relate other numbers in fact families.

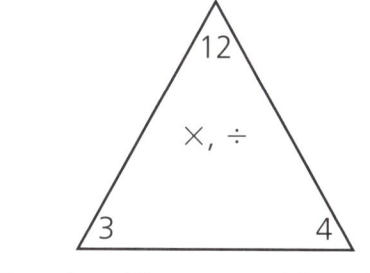

| $3 \times 4 = 12$ | $12 \div 4 = 3$ | $5 \times 7 = 35$ | $35 \div 7 = 5$ |
| $4 \times 3 = 12$ | $12 \div 3 = 4$ | $7 \times 5 = 35$ | $35 \div 5 = 7$ |

You can use fact families to solve division problems. For example, suppose you want to divide 20 by 5 but you do not know the answer.

$$20 \div 5 = \square$$

You can rewrite the division problem as a multiplication problem. Remember that the numbers you multiply together are called factors. In this problem, one of the factors is unknown.

$$5 \times \square = 20$$

> Use a letter or a shape to stand for an unknown number.

This number sentence says, "5 times what number is 20?" The answer is 4.

$$5 \times 4 = 20$$

UNIT 2 Operations and Algebraic Thinking, Part 1   **73**

Think About It

If you know one fact in a fact family, how can you find the rest of the facts?

_____

_____

_____

_____

Focused Instruction

Use an unknown factor, inverse operations, and repeated addition to solve a division problem.

Gunter has 36 baseball cards. He wants to divide them into 9 equal piles. How many cards should he place in each pile?

What number is Gunter dividing? _____

What number is Gunter dividing by? _____

Write a division problem to show this. Use a ☐ for the quotient.

_____

Rewrite the division problem as a multiplication problem.

_____

How many 9s does it take to make 36? Use repeated addition to find out. Show your addition.

_____

What is the unknown factor? _____

How many baseball cards should Gunter place in each pile? _____

Focused Instruction — Lesson 9

Use an unknown factor, inverse operations, and an array to solve a division problem.

Olga is planning a 30-mile bike ride. She wants to divide her ride so that she stops every 6 miles to drink 1 pint of water. How many pints of water will Olga need?

What are two numbers in the fact family that you need to find the answer?

_____ and _____

Write a multiplication problem with an unknown factor to show this problem.

_____

Make an array to find the unknown factor.

What is the unknown factor? _____

How many pints of water does Olga need? _____

Use what you know about unknown factors to answer these questions.

1. How can you rewrite 28 ÷ 4 = ☐ as a multiplication problem?

   _____

2. Write a division sentence made up of the numbers in the fact family 40, 8, and 5.

   _____

3. Write the division problem 34 ÷ 2 = ☐ as an unknown factor multiplication sentence.

   _____

UNIT 2 Operations and Algebraic Thinking, Part 1

Solve the following problems.

1. The array models a fact family.

   Part A What are the numbers in this fact family?

   Answer _____

   > Remember how the numbers in a fact family are related.

   Part B Write the multiplication and division sentences that relate the numbers in the fact family.

   _____

   _____

2. Explain how to use a multiplication sentence to solve $21 \div 3 = \square$.

   _____

   _____

   > Do not forget that multiplication and division are inverse operations.

Independent Practice

Lesson 9

Solve the following problems.

1 The multiplication sentence 7 × 6 = 42 is part of a fact family. Which of the following are other members of this fact family? Select the **three** correct answers.

A 42 − 6 = 36

B 42 ÷ 7 = 6

C 6 × 7 = 42

D 7 + 6 + 42 = 55

E 42 ÷ 6 = 7

2 Elijah wants to solve the division problem.

$$44 \div 4 = \square$$

Part A Rewrite the division problem as a multiplication problem.

Answer _____

Part B List the fact family Elijah can use.

_____

_____

3 Write the letter of the related multiplication problem from the box on the line after each division problem.

28 ÷ 4 = ☐ _____

32 ÷ 8 = ☐ _____

16 ÷ 4 = ☐ _____

48 ÷ 8 = ☐ _____

a	4 × ☐ = 16
b	8 × ☐ = 48
c	4 × ☐ = 28
d	8 × ☐ = 32

UNIT 2 Operations and Algebraic Thinking, Part 1

Independent Practice

4 Hamadi covered his driveway with square stones in rows. He used 56 stones. He put 7 stones in each row.

Part A Write a multiplication problem you could use to find the number of rows Hamadi made. Use a □ for the unknown factor.

Answer _____

Part B Fill in the missing numbers to complete the question asked in the multiplication problem.

What number can I multiply by _____ to get _____?

Part C How can you use a fact family to help you find the number of rows Hamadi made?

_____
_____

5 An array can model a multiplication sentence as well as a division sentence.

Part A Draw an array for 5 × 9 = 45. Write the rest of the fact family with one multiplication sentence and two division sentences.

Answer _____

Part B In a fact family, what happens to the quotient in a division fact when it is written as a multiplication fact?

_____
_____
_____

LESSON 10: Multiplication Facts

CCLS: 3.OA.4, 7

Part 1 Introduction

Basic multiplication facts are important to learn. You will use these facts as you learn more about multiplication and multiply bigger numbers.

Here are two important rules, or properties, that help you remember some facts:

- The **zero property:** any number multiplied by 0 is always 0.
- The **identity property:** any number multiplied by 1 is always itself.

$3 \times 0 = 0$ $\quad\quad$ $3 \times 1 = 3$
Zero Property $\quad\quad$ Identity Property

Mr. Gardner put some golf balls in some jars.

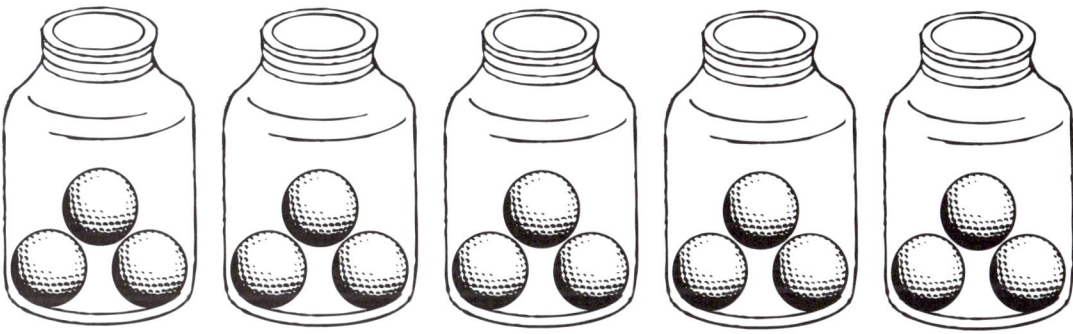

There are 5 jars. There are 3 golf balls. Use a basic multiplication fact to find how many golf balls there are in all.

$5 \times 3 = 15$ golf balls

Remember that division and multiplication are **inverse operations.** You can use division facts to help you find the answer to multiplication problems. You can use multiplication facts to help you find the answer to division problems.

In the picture above, there are 15 golf balls. They are divided evenly between 5 jars. You know that $5 \times 3 = 15$, so you also know that $15 \div 5 = 3$. There are 3 golf balls in each jar.

UNIT 2 Operations and Algebraic Thinking, Part 1

It is important for you to memorize basic multiplication facts. A multiplication table can help you learn them.

×	0	1	2	3	4	5	6	7	8	9
0	0	0	0	0	0	0	0	0	0	0
1	0	1	2	3	4	5	6	7	8	9
2	0	2	4	6	8	10	12	14	16	18
3	0	3	6	9	12	15	18	21	24	27
4	0	4	8	12	16	20	24	28	32	36
5	0	5	10	15	20	25	30	35	40	45
6	0	6	12	18	24	30	36	42	48	54
7	0	7	14	21	28	35	42	49	56	63
8	0	8	16	24	32	40	48	56	64	72
9	0	9	18	27	36	45	54	63	72	81

Think About It

What does it mean to say that division is the inverse operation of multiplication?

_____

_____

PART 2 Focused Instruction

Knowing and using multiplication facts help you answer questions.

Julia has 4 rows of cornstalks in her garden. Each row has 6 cornstalks. How many cornstalks are in Julia's garden?

Which numbers are known? _____

What are you trying to find out? _____

Write a multiplication sentence that you can use to find the answer. Use a box for the unknown number. _____

How many cornstalks are in Julia's garden? _____

Write a division sentence you can use to check your answer.

_____

Focused Instruction

Lesson 10

Look at this multiplication sentence.

$$6 \times \square = 42$$

What are the factors of the multiplication problem? _____

What is the product? _____

Write the problem as a division number sentence. _____

What number goes in the box? _____

How did the division problem help you find the missing factor?

_____

_____

Use what you know about multiplication to find the missing number in each of these multiplication sentences.

1 $5 \times$ _____ $= 50$

2 $3 \times 9 =$ _____

3 $7 \times 7 =$ _____

4 _____ $\times 2 = 16$

UNIT 2 Operations and Algebraic Thinking, Part 1

Guided Practice — Lesson 10

Solve the following problems.

1 How does knowing that 2 × 9 = 18 help you find the product of 4 × 9 without having to multiply?

How many times more than 2 is 4?

_____

_____

2 For a game, Chang places 54 cups in 9 rows.

Part A Write the multiplication sentence Chang could use to find the number of cups in each row. Use □ for the unknown number.

What parts of the multiplication sentence do you know?

Answer _____

Part B Write a division sentence you could use to find the number that goes in the box.

Answer _____

Part C How many cups did Chang put in each row?

Answer _____ cups

3 Judith made breakfast for 6 people. She had 2 muffins for each person.

Part A Write a multiplication sentence to find the total number of muffins. Use □ for the unknown number.

What numbers are the factors? What is the product?

Answer _____

Part B How many muffins did Judith have in all?

Answer _____ muffins

UNIT 2 Operations and Algebraic Thinking, Part 1

Solve the following problems.

1 Which of these facts has the same product as 3 × 4?

  A 5 × 2
  B 8 × 3
  C 2 × 6
  D 6 × 6

2 What is the missing number?

  4 × ☐ = 0

  A 4
  B 2
  C 1
  D 0

3 Look at the multiplication sentences below. Justin replaces the box in each sentence with an 8. Mark the correct box to show if each number sentence is true or false after Justin changes the box to an 8.

	True	False
8 × ☐ = 80	☐	☐
☐ × 1 = 8	☐	☐
2 × 4 = ☐	☐	☐
5 × ☐ = 58	☐	☐
0 × ☐ = 8	☐	☐
☐ × 7 = 56	☐	☐

UNIT 2 Operations and Algebraic Thinking, Part 1

Independent Practice

Lesson 10

4 Multiply:

10 × 0 = _____

5 Find the product.

5 × 5 = _____

6 What is the product of 10 and 4?

Answer _____

7 There are special relationships between multiplication and division.

Part A Explain how knowing 7 × 6 = 42 can help you find the quotient of 42 ÷ 6.

_____
_____
_____

Part B Travis multiplied 6 × 0 and got 0. Melia multiplied 6 × 0 and got 6. Who is correct? Explain.

_____
_____
_____
_____

Independent Practice

Lesson 10

8 A baker had this flat of eggs. She planned to use all the eggs to make cakes. She needed 3 eggs for each cake.

Part A The baker wrote this multiplication sentence to find the total number of eggs.

5 × 6 = ☐

How did the baker decide what factors to use?

_____

Part B How many eggs did the baker have in all?

Answer _____ eggs

Part C Next, the baker wrote the multiplication sentence 3 × ☐ = 30. What number goes in the box? Explain what the baker used this multiplication sentence to find out.

_____
_____

Lesson 11: Division Facts

Part 1 Introduction

Just like basic multiplication facts, basic division facts are important to know. As you learn more about math, you will need to know these basic facts to help you. Multiplication and division facts are related. When you know multiplication facts, you also know the related division facts.

Two important properties, or rules, will help you with some division facts:

- The **zero property:** 0 divided by any number is always 0. You cannot divide a number by 0.
- The **identity property:** any number, except 0, divided by itself is 1. Any number divided by 1 is that number.

$$0 \div 5 = 0 \qquad 36 \div 1 = 36 \qquad 36 \div 36 = 1$$
Zero Property $\qquad\qquad$ Identity Property

There are 25 roses. Melinda wants to make 5 bunches of roses.

Use a basic division fact to help you find how many roses will be in each bunch.

$$25 \div 5 = 5$$

There will be 5 roses in each bunch.

Remember that multiplication and division are inverse operations. You can use basic multiplication facts to help you find the answer to division problems.

In the problem above, if you know the basic multiplication fact $5 \times 5 = 25$, you can find the answer. There will be 5 roses in each bunch. There will be 5 bunches, so there are 25 roses in all.

Think About It

How are multiplication facts and division facts related in fact families? Give an example.

_____

_____

PART 2 Focused Instruction

Knowing division properties and facts can help you find missing values and solve problems.

Look at these division sentences.

A 9 ÷ 9 = ☐   **B** 0 ÷ 6 = ☐   **C** 34 ÷ 1 = ☐   **D** 16 ÷ 0 = ☐

Can you divide 0 into smaller parts? _____

Does dividing by 1 change the number you divide? _____

Which problem can you answer using the zero property? _____

Which problem can you answer by knowing that a number divided by itself is always 1? _____

Which problem can you answer by knowing that a number divided by 1 is the number itself? _____

Which problem cannot be done? _____

> Can you divide 0 by a number? Can you divide a number by 0?

Look at this division problem.

$$45 \div 9 = \square$$

Write the problem as a multiplication sentence with an unknown factor.

_____

How many total dots are in an array that models this problem? _____

How many rows of dots are in the array? _____

> Think about the fact family for this division sentence.

Focused Instruction — Lesson 11

How do you know when to stop adding rows of dots?
_____

How do you find the quotient from the array?
_____

Make the array.

What is 45 ÷ 9? _____

Use what you know about division to find the missing number in each of these division sentences.

1 0 ÷ 14 = _____

2 36 ÷ _____ = 6

3 27 ÷ 9 = _____

4 22 ÷ 1 = _____

Guided Practice

Solve the following problems.

1 Write each of these division sentences as multiplication sentences with an unknown factor. Then find the unknown number.

Part A 32 ÷ 4 = ☐

Multiplication Sentence _____

Unknown Number _____

When you rewrite division as multiplication, the quotient becomes one of the factors.

Part B 66 ÷ ☐ = 11

Multiplication Sentence _____

Unknown Number _____

Part C 56 ÷ 7 = ☐

Multiplication Sentence _____

Unknown Number _____

2 Jamal cut two pizzas into eight slices each for a total of 16 slices. The slices were divided equally among 4 people.

Part A Write a division sentence to show how many slices each person will get. Use ☐ for the quotient.

Answer _____

Think: How many 4s are in 16?

Part B What multiplication fact can help you find the quotient?

Answer _____

Part C How many slices did each person get?

Answer _____ slices

Remember that multiplication and division are inverse operations.

Independent Practice — Lesson 11

Solve the following problems.

1 What basic multiplication fact can help you divide 18 ÷ 3?

A 2 × 3 = 6

B 3 × 3 = 9

C 6 × 2 = 12

D 6 × 3 = 18

2 Fatima divided 63 by 9 and got a quotient of 6. Is she correct? Explain.

_____

_____

3 A worker is putting pieces of glass into windows. A window and one of the pieces of glass are shown here. The worker has 72 pieces of glass.

Part A Write the division sentence you could use to find the number of windows the worker can put glass in. Use □ for the unknown number.

Answer _____

Part B Write a multiplication fact you could use to find the answer to the division sentence in Part A.

Answer _____

Part C How many windows can the worker put glass into?

Answer _____ windows

Independent Practice — Lesson 11

4 Explain how you can use 6 × 9 = 54 to find 54 ÷ 9.

_____

_____

5 This array could be a model for a division sentence.

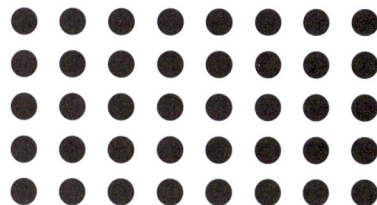

Part A Write two division sentences that the array could model.

Answer _____

Part B Write a multiplication sentence that you could use to find the answer to one of the division sentences in Part A.

Answer _____

6 Which of the following choices show a division sentence that has been correctly changed into a multiplication sentence? Select the **three** correct answers.

A 28 ÷ 7 = ☐ → 7 × ☐ = 28

B 39 ÷ ☐ = 39 → ☐ × 39 = 39

C 35 ÷ 5 = ☐ → 35 × ☐ = 5

D 42 ÷ ☐ = 7 → 7 × 7 = ☐

E 55 ÷ 5 = ☐ → 5 × ☐ = 55

LESSON 12: Patterns

CCLS: 3.OA.9

Part 1 Introduction

A **pattern** is an ordered set of numbers or objects that repeats or grows.

Look at this pattern.

5, 10, 15, 20, 25, 30, 35…

This pattern shows skip counting by 5s. Its rule is "add 5."

> A rule tells how the numbers in a pattern change.

Addition and multiplication facts have many patterns. You can find patterns by using addition and multiplication tables. Use an **addition table** to see what happens when you add odd and even numbers.

Is the sum of 3 + 4 even or odd?
Find the place where the column for 3 and the row for 4 meet on the table: 7. You can also look where the row for 3 and the column for 4 meet. The sum is the same.

> The commutative property of addition says you can add numbers in any order and the sum will be the same. The addition table helps you see that this is true.

The numbers in the rows and columns are addends. The place where the addends meet is the sum.

Addition Table

+	0	1	2	3	4	5	6	7	8	9
0	0	1	2	3	4	5	6	7	8	9
1	1	2	3	4	5	6	7	8	9	10
2	2	3	4	5	6	7	8	9	10	11
3	3	4	5	6	7	8	9	10	11	12
4	4	5	6	7	8	9	10	11	12	13
5	5	6	7	8	9	10	11	12	13	14
6	6	7	8	9	10	11	12	13	14	15
7	7	8	9	10	11	12	13	14	15	16
8	8	9	10	11	12	13	14	15	16	17
9	9	10	11	12	13	14	15	16	17	18

> Even numbers end in 0, 2, 4, 6, or 8.
> Odd numbers end in 1, 3, 5, 7, or 9.

Look at the other odd + even facts. All of the sums are odd. This is a pattern. When you add an odd number and an even number, the sum will always be an odd number.

Multiplication tables help you see more patterns with multiplication facts. You will do more with multiplication tables in Part 2.

UNIT 2 Operations and Algebraic Thinking, Part 1

Think About It

Think of a two-digit even number and a two-digit odd number. Add the numbers. Is the sum odd or even? Why do you think this is so?

_____

_____

Part 2 Focused Instruction

Multiplication tables help you see patterns in multiplication facts.

The top row and the first column show single-digit factors. The product is found where the factors **intersect**.

Multiplication Table

×	0	1	2	3	4	5	6	7	8	9
0	0	0	0	0	0	0	0	0	0	0
1	0	1	2	3	4	5	6	7	8	9
2	0	2	4	6	8	10	12	14	16	18
3	0	3	6	9	12	15	18	21	24	27
4	0	4	8	12	16	20	24	28	32	36
5	0	5	10	15	20	25	30	35	40	45
6	0	6	12	18	24	30	36	42	48	54
7	0	7	14	21	28	35	42	49	56	63
8	0	8	16	24	32	40	48	56	64	72
9	0	9	18	27	36	45	54	63	72	81

Circle the products for these number sentences in the table. Then write them in the answer spaces.

$1 \times 4 =$ _____ $3 \times 4 =$ _____

$5 \times 4 =$ _____ $7 \times 4 =$ _____

$9 \times 4 =$ _____

> Notice that each equation has 1 odd factor and 1 even factor.

What factor do all of these number sentences have? _____

Is this factor even or odd? _____

Are all of the products even, odd, or a mix of even and odd? _____

Why is the product always even when you multiply by 4? _____

_____

If you multiply 3×6, will the product be odd or even? _____

What is true about the product when one factor is even and one factor is odd?

_____

UNIT 2 Operations and Algebraic Thinking, Part 1

Focused Instruction

Lesson 12

Look for two even numbers on the multiplication table. Write a multiplication sentence with those two numbers. _____

Is the product even or odd? _____

Is this always true? Use two more multiplication problems to show that you are right.

_____

_____

Look at the multiplication table on the previous page. Find the column with 5 at the top.

When you multiply 5 × 2, you get 10. Next, multiply 5 × 3. See what happens as you move down the column. Find the next three products.

5 × 2 = 10   5 × 3 = 15

5 × 4 = _____   5 × 5 = _____

5 × 6 = _____

> The commutative property says you can multiply numbers in any order and the sum is the same.

What pattern do you notice when you look at the 5 column? Explain.

_____

_____

Use what you know about the addition and multiplication tables to answer these questions. Look back at the addition table on page 92 or at the multiplication table on page 93 if you need to.

1 What pattern do you see when you add 0 to any number?

_____

2 Look at the column for 9 in the multiplication table. Add the digits in each product for 9. What pattern do you see?

_____

_____

Guided Practice — Lesson 12

Solve the following problems.

1 Look at the multiplication table on page 93.

Part A Multiply.

0 × 2 = _____

4 × 0 = _____

1 × 6 = _____

9 × 1 = _____

Part B Think about your answers to Part A. Then finish these sentences.

> You can use the multiplication table to help you understand the properties of multiplication you learned about in Lesson 7.

If you multiply any number by 0, the product will always be _____.

Another example that shows this pattern is _____.

If you multiply any number by 1, the number _____.

An example of this pattern is _____.

2 Look at the addition table on page 92.

Part A Look at the sums when a number is added to itself. Then write the sums below.

2 + 2 = _____   3 + 3 = _____

4 + 4 = _____   5 + 5 = _____

6 + 6 = _____   7 + 7 = _____

8 + 8 = _____   9 + 9 = _____

Part B Look at the addition pattern. Circle the choice that completes each sentence.

When you add a number to itself, the sum is always [odd, even].

If the numbers you add are the same and they both go up by 1, the sum goes up by [1, 2, 4].

UNIT 2 Operations and Algebraic Thinking, Part 1

Independent Practice

Lesson 12

Solve the following problems.

Use the multiplication table to answer problems 1–4.

Multiplication Table

×	0	1	2	3	4	5	6	7	8	9
0	0	0	0	0	0	0	0	0	0	0
1	0	1	2	3	4	5	6	7	8	9
2	0	2	4	6	8	10	12	14	16	18
3	0	3	6	9	12	15	18	21	24	27
4	0	4	8	12	16	20	24	28	32	36
5	0	5	10	15	20	25	30	35	40	45
6	0	6	12	18	24	30	36	42	48	54
7	0	7	14	21	28	35	42	49	56	63
8	0	8	16	24	32	40	48	56	64	72
9	0	9	18	27	36	45	54	63	72	81

1 Look at the columns in the table above. In which column is each number 6 more than the number before it?

   A   the one with 1 at the top

   B   the one with 3 at the top

   C   the one with 6 at the top

   D   the one with 9 at the top

2 Look at the multiplication table above.

   Part A   Trista says that when one factor is even, the product is always even. Name a row that proves that Trista is correct.

   Answer _____

   Part B   Carter found a pattern in the multiplication table. He says that the product of 2 times any number can always be broken apart into two equal addends. Is Carter correct? Explain why or why not.

   _____
   _____
   _____
   _____

Independent Practice

3 Roger saves 3 dollars each day. Look at the row for 3. Which sentences are true about the row for 3? Select the **two** correct answers.

A The products are all even.

B Each number is 2 more than the number before it.

C Each number is 3 more than the number before it.

D There are both even and odd products.

E The products are all odd.

4 Karoline multiplied odd numbers by odd numbers. All of the answers were odd.

$3 \times 5 = 15$ $7 \times 1 = 7$ $1 \times 5 = 5$ $9 \times 5 = 45$

Part A Write another multiplication fact that shows Karoline's pattern.

Answer _____

Part B Would this pattern be true if Karoline added two odd numbers? Explain.

_____
_____
_____
_____

Independent Practice

Lesson 12

Use the addition table to answer problems 5 and 6.

Addition Table

+	0	1	2	3	4	5	6	7	8	9
0	0	1	2	3	4	5	6	7	8	9
1	1	2	3	4	5	6	7	8	9	10
2	2	3	4	5	6	7	8	9	10	11
3	3	4	5	6	7	8	9	10	11	12
4	4	5	6	7	8	9	10	11	12	13
5	5	6	7	8	9	10	11	12	13	14
6	6	7	8	9	10	11	12	13	14	15
7	7	8	9	10	11	12	13	14	15	16
8	8	9	10	11	12	13	14	15	16	17
9	9	10	11	12	13	14	15	16	17	18

5 Look at any column from top to bottom in the addition table above. What is the pattern?

A Add 1.

B Add 2.

C Add 9.

D Add 0.

6 Claude adds 2 to each number in the addition table. He notices that some of the sums are even.

Part A Add 2 to a number to find an even sum. Write the equation.

Answer _____

Part B Add 2 to a number to find an odd sum. Write the equation.

Answer _____

UNIT 2 Operations and Algebraic Thinking, Part 1

UNIT 2 REVIEW
Operations and Algebraic Thinking, Part 1

Solve the following problems.

1 Look at the addition table below.

Addition Table

+	0	1	2	3	4	5	6	7	8	9
0	0	1	2	3	4	5	6	7	8	9
1	1	2	3	4	5	6	7	8	9	10
2	2	3	4	5	6	7	8	9	10	11
3	3	4	5	6	7	8	9	10	11	12
4	4	5	6	7	8	9	10	11	12	13
5	5	6	7	8	9	10	11	12	13	14
6	6	7	8	9	10	11	12	13	14	15
7	7	8	9	10	11	12	13	14	15	16
8	8	9	10	11	12	13	14	15	16	17
9	9	10	11	12	13	14	15	16	17	18

Part A Lance looked at a column in the table above. He said that all the numbers in the column were even numbers. Is this possible? Explain why or why not.

_____

_____

Part B Lance looked at a row in the table. Then he looked at the column that started with the same number as the row. How are the row and column the same? What property does this show?

_____

_____

_____

_____

2 Use repeated subtraction to show how many groups of 7 are in 21. Then write a division sentence.

Answer _____

3 What number completes both number sentences?

$72 \div \square = 8 \qquad 8 \times \square = 72$

Answer _____

4 What is the product of 0 and 5? Explain how you know.

_____
_____

5 Write 5 + 5 + 5 + 5 + 5 + 5 = 30 as a multiplication sentence. Explain why you can do this.

_____
_____

6 Look at the multiplication table below.

Multiplication Table

×	0	1	2	3	4	5	6	7	8	9
0	0	0	0	0	0	0	0	0	0	0
1	0	1	2	3	4	5	6	7	8	9
2	0	2	4	6	8	10	12	14	16	18
3	0	3	6	9	12	15	18	21	24	27
4	0	4	8	12	16	20	24	28	32	36
5	0	5	10	15	20	25	30	35	40	45
6	0	6	12	18	24	30	36	42	48	54
7	0	7	14	21	28	35	42	49	56	63
8	0	8	16	24	32	40	48	56	64	72
9	0	9	18	27	36	45	54	63	72	81

Part A Find a column with an even number at the top. Describe the numbers in the column. Are the products even, odd, or both? Explain why.

_____

_____

Part B Find a column with an odd number at the top. Describe the numbers in the column. Are the numbers even, odd, or both? Explain why.

_____

_____

7 Write all the facts for the fact family with 3, 8, and 24.

Answer _____

UNIT 2 REVIEW Operations and Algebraic Thinking, Part 1

8 In which of these number sentences is the unknown number 7?
Select the **three** correct answers.

　　A　$4 \times \square = 28$

　　B　$42 \div 6 = \square$

　　C　$0 \div 7 = \square$

　　D　$81 \div \square = 9$

　　E　$36 \div 9 = \square$

　　F　$1 \times 7 = \square$

　　G　$7 \times \square = 14$

9 Use the distributive property to solve each of these problems.
Show your work.

　　A　$5 \times 17 = \square$

　　_____

　　B　$14 \times 7 = \square$

　　_____

　　C　$23 \times 4 = \square$

　　_____

　　D　$8 \times 12 = \square$

　　_____

10 What number is missing in this number sentence?

$$2 \times (6 \times 3) = (2 \times \square) \times 3$$

　　A　2

　　B　3

　　C　6

　　D　18

11. This array is the model for a fact family of three numbers.

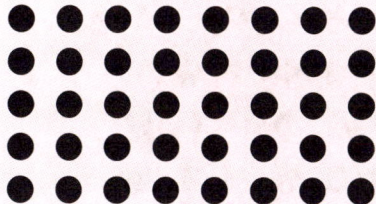

Part A Write the four members of the fact family.

_____
_____

Part B Choose one of the multiplication facts and explain how it is modeled by the array.

_____
_____

Part C Choose one of the division facts and explain how it is modeled by the array.

_____
_____

12. Find the product of 7 × 5.

   A 12

   B 28

   C 30

   D 35

13. Use the numbers 6, 4, and 2 to demonstrate the associative property of multiplication. Complete each equation.

   (6 × 4) × 2 = _____

   24 × 2 = _____

   48 = _____

UNIT 2 REVIEW Operations and Algebraic Thinking, Part 1

14 Look at the array below.

Part A Use the array to explain the commutative property.

_____
_____
_____

Part B Pete wants to use this array to show 4 × 6 = 24. Kirsten wants to use the array to show 24 ÷ 6 = 4. Is Pete correct, is Kirsten correct, or are both correct? Explain.

_____
_____
_____

15 Amy makes handmade dolls with yarn and buttons.

Part A One doll that Amy makes needs 6 buttons. She has 48 buttons in all. Does Amy have enough buttons to make 7 of these dolls? Explain.

_____
_____
_____

Part B Another doll that Amy makes needs 15 buttons. Amy wants to make 8 of these dolls. She has to multiply 8 × 15 to find how many buttons she needs. Explain how to find the product of 8 × 15 by using the distributive property.

_____
_____
_____

UNIT 3
Numbers and Operations in Base Ten

In Unit 2, you learned how to multiply, divide, and find patterns. Now you can use what you know about multiplication and division to round numbers and multiply by multiples of ten.

LESSON 13 Rounding Whole Numbers In this lesson, you will round numbers up or down to the nearest ten or nearest hundred.

LESSON 14 Adding Whole Numbers In this lesson, you will add by regrouping and using place-value charts.

LESSON 15 Subtracting Whole Numbers In this lesson, you will subtract by regrouping and using place-value charts.

LESSON 16 Multiplying by Multiples of Ten In this lesson, you will multiply using the associative property and place-value models.

LESSON 13: Rounding Whole Numbers

CCLS: 3.NBT.1

Part 1 Introduction

Rounding is useful when you do not need an exact number. When you round, you find a number that is close to a number, but not exactly the same. The Rojas family took a trip. They drove 483 miles. They say that the trip was about 500 miles. They rounded the number of miles. The word *about* is often a clue to let you know a number was rounded.

Giselle will round 274 to the nearest hundred. To round to the nearest hundred, look at the digit in the place to the right. The place to the right of the hundreds place is the tens place. If the digit is 5 or greater, round up. If the digit is less than 5, round down. The digit in the tens place of Giselle's number is 7. So Giselle will round up to the next hundred.

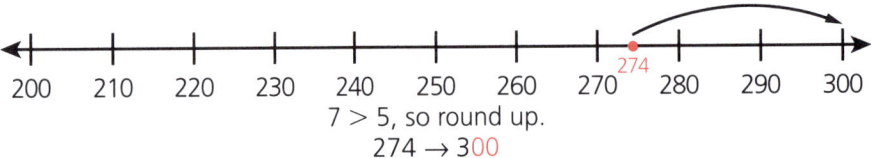

7 > 5, so round up.
274 → 300

> The digits in the places to the right of the place you round to are replaced with 0s.

The number line shows that 274 is closer to 300 than it is to 200. So it makes sense to round to 300.

Giselle will round 274 to the nearest ten instead. To round to the nearest ten, look at the digit in the place to the right. The place to the right of the tens place is the ones place. If the digit is 5 or greater, round up. If the digit is less than 5, round down.

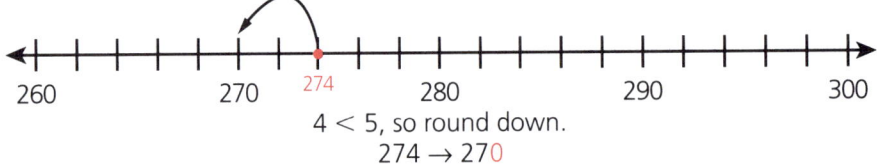

4 < 5, so round down.
274 → 270

The number line shows that 274 is closer to 270 than it is to 280. So it makes sense to round to 270.

UNIT 3 Numbers and Operations in Base Ten

Think About It

Nigel rounds a three-digit number to the nearest hundreds place: 300. Think of a number Nigel could have rounded up and a number he could have rounded down. Explain how you arrived at these answers.

_____

_____

_____

_____

Part 2 Focused Instruction

The rules for rounding are true for any number.

The town of Seaside has 1,437 people. About how many people live in Seaside?

First, round to the nearest ten.

What place is to the right of the tens place? _____

What digit is in the place to the right of the tens place? _____

Is the digit greater than or equal to 5? _____

Should you round up or down? _____

> Use the digit to the right of the place value you are rounding to.

In the rounded number,

Does the thousands digit change? If so, to what? _____

Does the hundreds digit change? If so, to what? _____

Does the tens digit change? If so, to what? _____

Does the ones digit change? If so, to what? _____

Rounded to the nearest ten, about how many people live in Seaside?

_____

Check your answer using the number line.

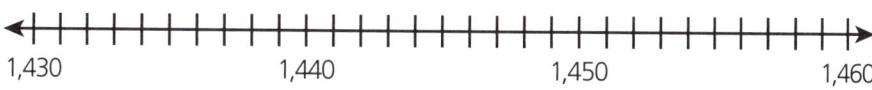

Focused Instruction — Lesson 13

Next, round to the nearest hundred.

What place is to the right of the hundreds place? _____

What digit is in the place to the right of the hundreds place? _____

Is the digit greater than or equal to 5? _____

Should you round up or down? _____

In the rounded number,

    Does the thousands digit change? If so, to what? _____

    Does the hundreds digit change? If so, to what? _____

    Does the tens digit change? If so, to what? _____

    Does the ones digit change? If so, to what? _____

About how many people live in Seaside rounded to the nearest hundred?

_____

Check your answer using a number line.

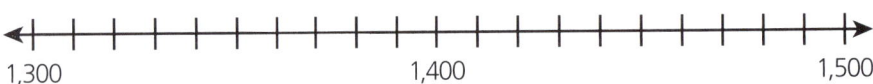

Use what you know about rounding to round each number to the nearest ten and hundred.

Number	Rounded to Nearest Ten	Rounded to Nearest Hundred
147		
163		
822		
3,285		

Guided Practice

Solve the following problems.

1 Diego's family has 327 books.

Part A Round 327 to the nearest ten.

Answer _____

> Remember to change all digits to the right of the place being rounded to 0.

Part B Round 327 to the nearest hundred.

Answer _____

Part C Which is greater, rounding 327 to the nearest ten or hundred? Explain why.

_____
_____
_____

2 Erica took pictures on her vacation. When she rounds the number of pictures to the nearest hundred, it is 600. When she rounds the number to the nearest ten, it is 570.

Part A What could be the number of pictures Erica took?

Answer _____

> Do not forget that many different numbers can round to the same number.

Part B Explain why your answer is correct.

_____
_____
_____
_____

Part 4 Independent Practice — Lesson 13

Solve the following problems.

1 Round 3,447 to the nearest hundred.

    A 3,400

    B 3,447

    C 3,450

    D 3,500

2 Ms. Lee cuts 982 squares out of paper for an art project.

    Part A Round 982 to the nearest ten.

              Answer _____

              How many digits are in the new number? Circle: 3   4

    Part B Round 982 to the nearest hundred.

              Answer _____

              How many digits are in the new number? Circle: 3   4

3 Carlos rounds the number of blocks in a classroom to the nearest ten. He says there are about 650 blocks in the classroom. Which numbers could be the exact number of blocks? Select the **three** correct answers.

    A 653

    B 661

    C 635

    D 644

    E 645

    F 648

Independent Practice

Lesson 13

4 What is 1,049 rounded to the nearest hundred?

Answer _____

5 Avery rounds some numbers to the nearest ten and hundred. Match the **exact** numbers to the **rounded** numbers. Write the exact numbers in the column. Not all of Avery's numbers will go in the table.

Avery's Numbers:							
356	422	874	1,045	1,053	3,214	3,196	3,221

Exact Number	Nearest Ten	Nearest Hundred
	360	400
	870	900
	1,050	1,100
	3,200	3,200

6 Which number does **not** round to 1,700 when rounded to the nearest hundred?

A 1,654

B 1,682

C 1,749

D 1,750

7 There were 473 people at the opening night of the drama club's play. Alessandra told Rashad that "about 500" people came to see the play that night. Is this true? Explain.

_____

_____

_____

UNIT 3 Numbers and Operations in Base Ten

Independent Practice — Lesson 13

8 Nathan has 2,085 inches of yarn. He tells his mom that he has about 2,090 inches of yarn.

Part A Did Nathan round to the nearest ten or hundred?

Answer _____

Part B Explain how you know your answer to Part A is correct.

_____

_____

9 A radio station played 2,874 different songs one year. About how many different songs did the station play in the year? Round to the nearest hundred.

Answer _____ songs

Lesson 14: Adding Whole Numbers

CCLS: 3.NBT.2

Part 1 Introduction

When you **add**, you join at least two numbers. Adding gives you a total that is larger than the numbers that you join together. The numbers you are adding are called **addends**. The result is called the **sum**. The order you add the numbers does not matter. The sum will remain the same.

Sometimes when you add, you need to **regroup**. You must regroup when the sum of a place is 10 or more. You always regroup numbers as the next place value to the left. So, you regroup 10 ones as 1 ten or 10 tens as 1 hundred. Use **place value** to help you regroup.

Add. 24
     +47

Add the ones.
Regroup 10 ones as ten.
Then, add the tens.

24
+47
———
71

The sum of 24 + 47 is 71.

Think About It

Marcus wants to add 174 + 248. Will Marcus have to regroup at all while adding? If so, in which places will he have to regroup? Explain how you know when you need to regroup when adding.

_____
_____
_____
_____

UNIT 3 Numbers and Operations in Base Ten

Focused Instruction

Lesson 14

Add to find the total. Use the place-value chart to help you.

Noah wants to know the total number of fans at the soccer game Friday and Saturday nights. Friday night, there were 276 fans, and Saturday night, there were 358 fans. How many fans were at both soccer games?

```
  276
+ 358
```

Hundreds	Tens	Ones
___	___	
2	7	6
+ 3	5	8
___	___	___

Add the ones. _____

Do you need to regroup the ones? _____

If so, how will you regroup? Complete the sentence below.

Regroup _____ ones into _____ ten(s) and _____ one(s).

Write the correct digits in the ones place and above the tens place.

Now add the tens. _____

Do you need to regroup the tens? _____

If so, how will you regroup? Complete the sentence below.

Regroup _____ tens into _____ hundred(s) and _____ ten(s).

> Regroup when you have more than 10 in a place.

Write the correct digits in the tens place and above the hundreds place.

Now add the hundreds. _____

Do you need to regroup the hundreds? _____

How many fans were at Friday and Saturday's soccer games? _____

Would your answer change if there were 358 fans on Friday and 276 fans on Saturday? Explain why or why not.

_____

_____

 **Focused Instruction** Lesson 14

Sometimes you must add more than two numbers. Align the numbers correctly to add.

Three third-grade classes were having a contest to see who could recycle the most paper. Mr. Welsh's class gathered 147 pounds of paper, Mr. Caminitti's class gathered 181 pounds of paper, and Mrs. Long's class gathered 153 pounds of paper. How many pounds of paper did the three classes gather for recycling?

How many pounds of paper did each class gather?

Mr. Welsh's class _____ pounds

Mr. Caminitti's class _____ pounds

Mrs. Long's class _____ pounds

Write these three numbers in the space at the right.
Be sure to line up the correct place values.

Add the ones. When do you regroup a place?

_____

Do you need to regroup the ones? _____

Add the tens. Do you need to regroup the tens? _____

Add the hundreds. Do you need to regroup the hundreds? _____

How many pounds of paper did the three classes gather? _____

Use what you know about adding to find these sums.

1 54 + 43 = _____

2 412 + 529 = _____

3 167 + 85 = _____

UNIT 3 Numbers and Operations in Base Ten

Guided Practice — Lesson 14

Solve the following problems.

1. Sheila added 494 + 208. Her work and the sum she found are shown below.

   ```
     1
    494
   +208
   ────
    602
   ```

   > Remember to regroup when you have more than 10 ones or tens.

   Part A What mistake did Sheila make?

   _____

   _____

   Part B Find the correct sum. Show your work.

   Answer _____

2. Add 483 + 377. Show your work.

   > Sometimes you need to regroup more than once.

   Answer _____

116 UNIT 3 Numbers and Operations in Base Ten

Part 4 Independent Practice — Lesson 14

Solve the following problems.

1 Add: 92
       +368

  A 350

  B 360

  C 450

  D 460

2 What is the sum of 76 and 25?

  A 91

  B 101

  C 111

  D 191

3 Edmund used a place-value chart to add 397 + 525.

Hundreds	Tens	Ones
5	2	5
3	9	7

Which digit should Edmund write in the tens place?

  A 0

  B 1

  C 2

  D 7

UNIT 3 Numbers and Operations in Base Ten

Independent Practice

Lesson 14

4 Steve's Sandwich Shop adds up their sales for the week. They sold $373 in ham sandwiches, $273 in roast beef, $419 in turkey, and $194 in meatball sandwiches. Which two kinds of sandwiches together sold $467 for the week?

   A ham and meatball

   B turkey and meatball

   C ham and roast beef

   D meatball and roast beef

5 To find the sum of 395 and 477, do you need to regroup once or twice? Explain your answer.

   _____

   _____

6 Add 38 + 567. Show your work.

   Answer _____

UNIT 3 Numbers and Operations in Base Ten

7 Tia used place-value blocks to solve 409 + 298.

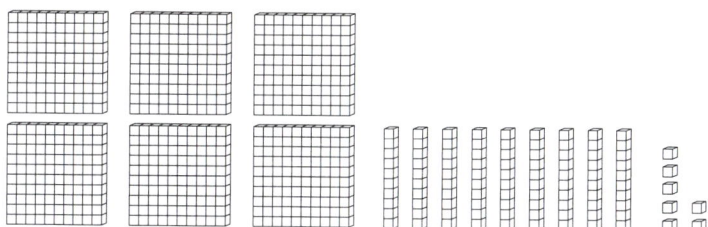

Part A Is Tia's model correct? Explain why or why not.

_____

_____

_____

_____

Part B If Tia's model is not correct, draw place-value blocks to model the correct answer. If it is correct, write *correct* below.

LESSON 15

Subtracting Whole Numbers

CCLS: 3.NBT.2

 **Introduction**

When you **subtract,** you take one number away from another. Subtracting gives you a total that is less than at least one of the numbers that you started with. The answer to a subtraction problem is called the **difference.**

Sometimes when you subtract, you need to **regroup.** When you regroup, you rename a number that is too small to subtract from. Unlike regrouping in addition, you regroup from left to right when you subtract. You regroup 1 hundred into 10 tens and 1 ten into 10 ones. Use place-value models to help you understand regrouping.

Subtract.   86
            −47

First, subtract the ones. You cannot subtract 7 from 6. So you must regroup 1 ten as 10 ones. Then add the 10 ones to the ones you already have.

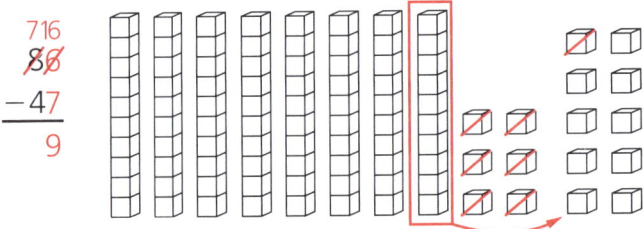

Then, subtract the tens:

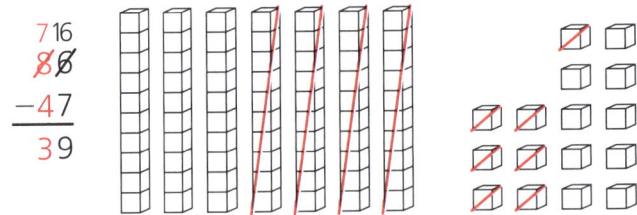

Look at the blocks that are not crossed out. The difference of 86 − 47 is 39.

Think About It

Explain how you know when you need to regroup in subtraction.

_____

_____

PART 2 Focused Instruction

A place-value chart can help you regroup and subtract.

There were 427 people at a carnival for the third-grade night. On the fourth-grade night, there were 364 people. How many more people were at the third-grade night of the carnival?

Hundreds	Tens	Ones
4 − 3	2 6	7 4

Do you need to regroup to subtract the ones? _____

Subtract the ones. _____

Do you need to regroup to subtract the tens? _____

If so, how will you regroup? Complete the sentence below.

Regroup _____ hundreds into _____ hundred(s) and

_____ ten(s).

Write the correct digits above the hundreds place and above the tens place.

Now subtract the tens. _____

Do you need to regroup the hundreds? _____

Subtract the hundreds. _____

How many more people were at the third-grade night than the fourth-grade night? _____

> In subtraction, regroup from left to right.

Part 2 Focused Instruction — Lesson 15

Sometimes you have to subtract across zeros. You will need to regroup more than once before you can subtract. Answer these questions to help you subtract across zeros.

Subtract: 500
         −143

Can you subtract the digits in the ones place? Why or why not?

_____

Can you regroup the tens place to subtract the ones? Why or why not?

_____

Regroup the hundreds place. Complete the following sentence.

Regroup 5 hundreds as _____ hundred(s) and _____ ten(s).

Now regroup the tens so you can subtract the ones. Complete the following sentence.

> Move to the left until there is a place you can regroup.

Regroup _____ ten(s) as _____ ten(s) and _____ one(s).

Subtract the ones. _____ − _____ = _____

Subtract the tens. _____ − _____ = _____

Subtract the hundreds. _____ − _____ = _____

What is the difference? _____

Use what you know about subtracting to find these differences.

1 305 − 122 = _____

2 754 − 314 = _____

3 488 − 97 = _____

122 **UNIT 3 Numbers and Operations in Base Ten**

**Guided Practice** — Lesson 15

Solve the following problems.

1 Kahrae used a place-value chart to subtract 714 − 483.

Hundreds	Tens	Ones
7	11 ̶1̶	4
− 4	8	3
3	3	1

Part A Is his answer correct? Why or why not?

_____

_____

Part B Find the difference. Show your work.

> Sometimes you need to regroup more than once.

Answer _____

2 Owen's team had 143 hockey games over the last three years. Owen played in 127 games. How many hockey games did Owen miss? Show your work.

> Regroup from left to right.

Answer _____ games

Part 4 Independent Practice — Lesson 15

Solve the following problems.

1 Subtract: 800
            −427

   A 373
   B 383
   C 473
   D 483

2 Subtract 63 − 37.

   A 23
   B 25
   C 26
   D 36

3 The number of people at a pool each day is shown in the table below.

PEOPLE AT POOL

Day	Number of People
Monday	147
Tuesday	219
Wednesday	271
Thursday	304
Friday	322

For which two days was there a difference of 103 people?

   A Monday and Thursday
   B Wednesday and Thursday
   C Tuesday and Friday
   D Monday and Tuesday

Independent Practice

Lesson 15

4 To find the difference between 811 and 634, do you need to regroup once or twice? Explain your answer.

_____

_____

_____

_____

5 Roseanne is subtracting numbers from 725. She knows that sometimes she has to regroup twice. For which of the numbers below would Roseanne **not** need to regroup twice when she subtracts it from 725? Select the **three** correct answers.

- **A** 146
- **B** 304
- **C** 539
- **D** 612
- **E** 632
- **F** 637

6 Subtract 600 − 137. Show your work.

Answer _____

UNIT 3 Numbers and Operations in Base Ten

Independent Practice — Lesson 15

7 Tammi used place-value blocks to solve 678 − 298.

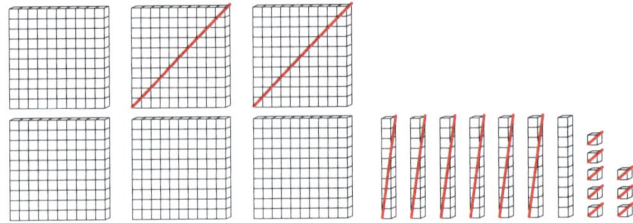

Part A Why is Tammi's model **not** correct? Explain.

_____

_____

_____

_____

Part B Draw place-value blocks to model the correct answer.

Part C How can Tammi use addition to check her answer?

_____

_____

_____

LESSON 16: Multiplying by Multiples of Ten

CCLS: 3.NBT.3

Part 1 Introduction

A **multiple** is a number you get when you multiply a number by any other number. So, multiples of 10 are 10, 20, 30, 40, 50, and so on. You can use different ways to multiply numbers by multiples of 10.

You can use place-value models to multiply multiples of 10.

Multiply 4 × 30. Model the number 30 with place-value blocks. Then show it 3 times. Count by tens.

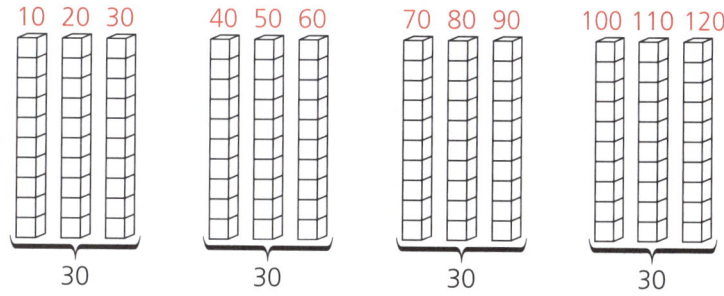

So, 4 groups of 3 tens is 120, or 4 × 30 = 120.

You can also multiply using a basic fact and then add a 0.

To multiply 4 × 30, think of the basic fact 4 × 3. You know 4 × 3 = 12. Add one zero to the end of the number because there is one zero in the multiple of 10. So 4 × 30 = 120.

Use the **associative property**.

Look at the problem 4 × 30.

You can break 30 into 3 × 10. Now the problem becomes 4 × (3 × 10).

Move the parentheses so the problem is (4 × 3) × 10. You know the basic fact 4 × 3 = 12. Multiply the basic fact by 10: 12 × 10 = 120.

So the product is 120.

> The associative property of multiplication says you can group numbers in any order to multiply.

UNIT 3 Numbers and Operations in Base Ten

Think About It

An ATM at a bank gives $20 bills. Henry used the machine to get 5 $20 bills. How much money did Henry get from the bank? Explain how you found the answer.

_____

_____

_____

_____

PART 2 Focused Instruction

Multiply. Draw place-value blocks to help you.

A train is traveling at 50 miles per hour. How many miles will the train travel in 4 hours?

What is the multiplication problem you need to solve?

_____

Draw tens blocks to show the multiple of 10 in this problem.

> Think about the number that is multiplied by 10.

How many groups of tens blocks do you need to find the answer? _____

In the space above, draw the groups of tens blocks you need to find the answer.

How many miles will the train travel in 4 hours? _____

128 UNIT 3 Numbers and Operations in Base Ten

 **Focused Instruction** — Lesson 16

Multiply. Use the associative property to help you.

Jazy entered a bike race. He needs to ride 500 miles to get to the finish line. He plans to ride 60 miles a day for 8 days. If he sticks to his plan, will Jazy make it to the finish line in 8 days? Explain.

What is the multiplication problem you need to solve?

_____

How can you break apart the multiple of 10? _____

Rewrite the problem with the multiple of 10 broken apart.

_____

Use the associative property to rewrite the problem using the basic fact. _____

What is the product of the basic fact? _____

> Use what you know about basic multiplication facts.

Add a zero to the end of your basic fact. What number do you have now?

_____

Will Jazy reach the finish line if he rides 60 miles a day for 8 days? Explain why or why not.

_____
_____
_____

Use what you know about multiplying multiples of 10 to answer these questions.

1. What is 5 × 60? _____

2. Multiply: 3 × 90 = _____

3. Mrs. West bought 4 packs of colored pencils. Each pack has 20 pencils. How many pencils did Mrs. West buy in all?

_____

PART 3 Guided Practice

Solve the following problems.

1 Desmond has 7 packs of cards. Each pack has 30 cards in it. Desmond knows he can break apart the multiple of 10 to help him multiply. He writes the problem shown below. He is stuck and does not know what to do next.

$$7 \times (2 \times 15) = (7 \times 2) \times 15 = 14 \times 15$$

Part A Is there an easier way for Desmond to multiply? Explain.

_____

_____

_____

> What is the best way to break apart a multiple of 10?

Part B Find the number of cards Desmond has. Show all your work.

Answer _____ cards

2 Chuck moved some crates of potatoes. The potatoes were packed in 10-pound bags. There were 9 bags of potatoes in each crate. Chuck moved 9 crates from a truck to a warehouse.

Part A How many pounds of potatoes are in each crate?

Answer _____ pounds

> Find the number of bags in each crate. How much does one bag weigh?

Part B Use the associative property to find the number of pounds of potatoes Chuck moved from the truck to the warehouse. Show your work.

Answer _____ pounds

130 UNIT 3 Numbers and Operations in Base Ten

© The Continental Press, Inc.   DUPLICATING THIS MATERIAL IS ILLEGAL.

Independent Practice — Lesson 16

Solve the following problems.

1 Daysia collects stamps. She keeps them in stamp collector's books. She has 3 books, and each book has 80 stamps. Daysia says she has 24 stamps. Is she correct?

   A Yes, Daysia multiplied correctly.

   B No, Daysia should add 3 and 80.

   C No, Daysia should subtract 3 from 80.

   D No, Daysia should add a 0 to the end of the basic fact.

2 The marching band needs 7 cases of water. Each case has 40 bottles in it. How many bottles of water does the marching band need?

   Answer _____ bottles

3 Faith multiplied a number by a multiple of 10. She used the associative property to help.

$$4 \times (7 \times 10) = (4 \times 7) \times 10$$

   Which shows the multiplication problem Faith solved?

   A 4×70

   B 11×10

   C 3×10

   D 11×4

4 A recipe calls for 20 ounces of chicken broth. A chef is making 9 batches of this recipe. How many ounces of chicken broth will she need?

   Answer _____ ounces

Independent Practice — Lesson 16

5 Which multiplication problems are correct? Select the **three** correct answers.

- A $6 \times 60 = 360$
- B $30 \times 8 = 240$
- C $9 \times 40 = 940$
- D $5 \times 80 = 560$
- E $40 \times 6 = 400$
- F $8 \times 80 = 640$

6 Lucy paints dolls to sell at a fair. So far, Lucy has painted the fingers and toes of 8 dolls. How many fingers and toes did Lucy paint? Write your number sentence and the product.

Answer _____ fingers and toes

7 Adam wants to solve 50×8.

Part A What basic fact should Adam use to find the product?

Answer _____

Part B Find the product.

Answer _____

8 Jason can order rolls in batches of 40 from a baker. He needs 280 rolls for a family reunion. Jason plans to order 6 batches of rolls. Will this be enough rolls? If not, how many batches should Jason order? Explain.

_____
_____
_____
_____

UNIT 3 Numbers and Operations in Base Ten

UNIT 3 REVIEW
Number and Operations in Base Ten

CCLS: 3.NBT.1–3

1. Which numbers round to 2,100 when rounded to the nearest hundred? Select the **two** correct answers.

   A   2,049

   B   2,149

   C   2,150

   D   2,009

   E   2,109

2. Subtract 399 from 501. Show your work.

   Answer _____

3. Zoe multiplied 6 × 50 = 300. Why are there two zeros in the product?
   _____
   _____

4 Look at the addition number sentence below.

$$455 + 149 = \square$$

Part A Add 455 to 149. Then round the sum to the nearest ten. Show your work.

Answer _____

Part B Round 455 and 149 to the nearest tens. Then add the sums. Show your work.

Answer _____

5 Parker wants to find the difference between 800 and 378.

Part A Subtract 800 − 378. Show your work.

Answer _____

Part B How can you use addition to check your answer in Part A?
_____
_____

6 Subtract 504 − 198.

    A 306

    B 316

    C 406

    D 416

7 Find the product of 6 × 60.

    A 360

    B 366

    C 420

    D 660

8 The distance from Javier's house to his grandparents' house is 372 miles. He thinks this is about 300 miles. Is this correct? Explain.

_____

_____

9 Mrs. Turner wrote these directions on the board.

- Subtract 154 from 395. Then round the difference to the nearest ten.
- Round 154 and 395 to the nearest ten. Then find the difference.

Chris followed these directions. Which set of directions will give Chris a larger number? Show your work.

Answer _____

10 Natalya subtracted 461 from 740. Her work is below.

$$\begin{array}{r} 6\,14\,10 \\ 7\,4\,0 \\ -\,4\,6\,1 \\ \hline 2\,8\,9 \end{array}$$

Part A What mistake did Natalya make?

_____

_____

_____

Part B Find the difference. Show your work.

Answer _____

11 Which of the following number sentences are correct? Select the **three** correct answers.

A 4 × 80 = 320

B 5 × 10 = 500

C 6 × 90 = 540

D 4 × 30 = 70

E 3 × 30 = 90

F 2 × 60 = 80

12 Danielle lives 5 miles from her cousins. She lives 30 times as far from her grandparents. How far from her grandparents does Danielle live?

Answer _____ miles

13 Lacey used a basic multiplication fact to multiply 8 × 30. What basic fact did Lacey use? Find the product of 8 × 30.

Answer _____

14 Subtract 139 from 390. Round the answer to the nearest ten and the nearest hundred.

Nearest Ten _____

Nearest Hundred _____

15 The table below shows the height in feet of five of the world's tallest buildings.

BUILDING HEIGHTS

Building	Height (ft)
A	2,717
B	1,667
C	1,614
D	1,588
E	1,483

Part A What is the height of building A rounded to the nearest ten?

Answer _____

Part B Which two buildings have the same height when rounded to the nearest hundred? What is that rounded height?

Answer _____

UNIT 4
Operations and Algebraic Thinking, Part 2

In Unit 2, you learned that repeated addition and repeated subtraction are called multiplication and division. Now you can use what you know about multiplying and dividing to solve one- and two-step word problems.

LESSON 17 One-Step Word Problems with Multiplication and Division In this lesson, you will use fact families and arrays to solve word problems. You will also use symbols to change word problems into number sentences to solve one-step problems.

LESSON 18 Two-Step Word Problems In this lesson, you will write expressions and equations to represent two-step word problems. You will also solve two-step word problems following the order of operations.

LESSON 17: One-Step Word Problems with Multiplication and Division

CCLS: 3.OA.3

Part 1 Introduction

You can write math sentences called **equations** to solve word problems. Numbers combined with symbols for operations, such as 3 × 8, are called **expressions.** An equation is a number sentence that shows two expressions are equal. Look for words that are clues that tell you what to write.

In word problems, look for words that give you clues about what to do.

> A farmer has 27 pigs. He wants to put equal groups of pigs into 3 pens. How many pigs should the farmer put in each pen?

> The farmer wants "equal groups," so use division. Think about what you are trying to find out: the number of pigs in each pen. Let p stand for this number. Then write a number sentence to help you find the answer. You can find p by dividing 27 by 3.

$$27 \div 3 = p$$
$$9 = p$$

> The farmer will put 9 pigs in each pen.

Word Clues

Multiplication
- multiply
- times
- groups of

Divide
- divide
- equal groups
- share
- split equally

Sometimes you can make an array to help you find the answer to a word problem. This array helps you solve the problem above. There are 9 pigs in each row.

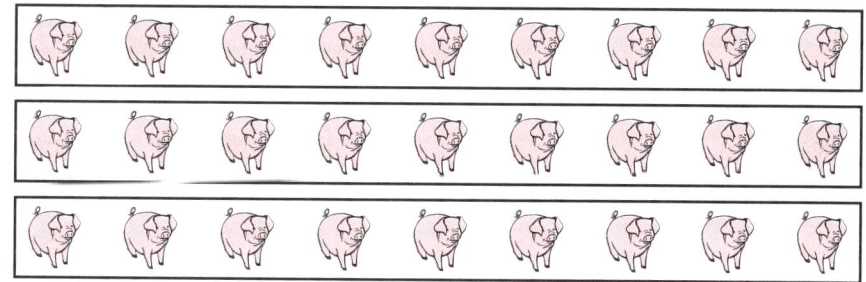

Use inverse operations when you solve problems.

> Kamilia is twice as old as her brother Jacek. If Kamilia is 10, how old is Jacek?

> Use a letter to show Jacek's age: b. "Twice as old as her brother" means "two times her brother's age": $2 \times b$.

Think of the word *is* as an equal sign (=).

UNIT 4 Operations and Algebraic Thinking, Part 2   **139**

Kamilia is 10, so $2 \times b = 10$.

Rewrite the multiplication sentence as a division sentence: $10 \div 2 = b$.

So $b = 5$, which means that Jacek is 5 years old.

> Multiplication and division are inverse operations.

Think About It

Measure the width of your classroom in steps. Count how many steps you take when you cross the room. Write and solve a division sentence that tells the length of one of your steps.

_____

_____

PART 2 Focused Instruction

Use symbols to change a word problem into a number sentence. Then solve the number sentence to find the answer. Pay attention to what the word problem is asking.

A school bus holds 36 students when it is full. Each row of seats holds 4 students. How many rows of seats does this bus have?

What is the total number of students on the bus? _____

What factors can be multiplied to give the product? _____

Write the multiplication sentence. Use r for the unknown.

_____

Division and multiplication are inverse operations. When a multiplication sentence is changed into a division sentence, what does the product become?

_____

Write the division sentence that is the inverse of the multiplication sentence you wrote above. _____

How many rows of seats are in the school bus? _____

Focused Instruction — Lesson 17

It takes Cindy 2 hours to drive to her favorite campground. It takes 3 times as long to drive to her favorite beach. How long does it take Cindy to drive to her favorite beach?

What are you trying to find out? _____

Write a letter to use for this number. _____

How many hours does it take Cindy to drive to the campground? _____

What words compare this time with how long it takes to drive to the beach?

_____

What operation do these words tell you to do?

_____

Write a number sentence to show this word problem. _____

How many hours does it take Cindy to drive to the beach? _____

Use what you know about word problems to answer these questions.

1. Rhonda has 45 beads. She uses 9 to make a necklace. Write a number sentence to find how many necklaces Rhonda can make with 45 beads.

   _____

2. There are 8 dogs at a dog park. Rosa gives 3 treats to each dogs. Write and solve a number sentence to find the total number of treats Rosa gave the dogs.

   _____

UNIT 4 Operations and Algebraic Thinking, Part 2

Solve the following problems.

1 Bayo's cat eats 2 cans of cat food every week. There are 14 cans of cat food on a shelf. How many weeks will the cat food last?

Part A Write a multiplication sentence for this problem. Use *w* for the unknown number.

Answer _____

Think about what the unknown represents.

Part B Write a division sentence for the problem.

Answer _____

Part C How many weeks will the cat food last?

Answer _____ weeks

2 José is 30 years old. He is 5 times as old as his son, Luis.

Part A Write a multiplication sentence you can use to find Luis's age. Use *a* for Luis's age.

Answer _____

What basic fact can you use to find the value of a?

Part B How old is Luis?

Answer _____ years old

3 A farmer planted 24 olive trees in a field. He planted the trees in rows of 6.

Part A Draw an array to show the olive trees that the farmer planted.

How many rows are in the array?

Part B How many rows of trees did the farmer plant?

Answer _____ rows

Independent Practice

Solve the following problems.

1. A farm stand has twice as many ears of corn as pumpkins. If there are 48 ears of corn, how many pumpkins are there?

   A 2
   B 24
   C 50
   D 96

2. Packs of gum have 8 pieces each. Pam wants to buy 56 pieces of gum. How many packs should she buy? Write an equation to find the answer. Use g for the number of packs. Solve the equation.

   Answer _____

3. Trudy read the following problem.

   Andrea and Bill are ushers at a theater. Andrea has taken 3 times as many tickets as Bill. Andrea took 15 tickets. How many tickets did Bill take?

   Trudy wrote the equation $3 \times 15 = n$, where n is the number of tickets Bill has taken. She says Bill took 45 tickets. Is she correct? Explain.

   _____
   _____
   _____

Independent Practice — Lesson 17

4 Some swim teams traveled to a swim meet. Each team had 9 swimmers. A total of 54 swimmers went to the meet.

Part A Write a number sentence to show how many teams went to the meet. Use *s* for the unknown number. Then solve for *s*.

Answer _____

Part B There were twice as many boys as there were girls at the meet. If 36 boys went to the meet, how many girls went to the meet?

Answer _____ girls

5 A worker wants to place 24 cans of soup on shelves. He wants to have 3 or more rows of cans. He does not want to have more than 8 cans in a row. Each row must have the same number of cans.

Part A Make two arrays to show how the worker could place the cans on the shelves.

Part B Write a multiplication sentence for each array to show that they will equal 24 cans.

Answer _____

6 Jared makes square picture frames. The frame is shown in the picture below.

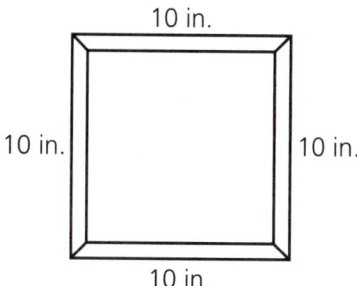

Part A How many picture frames can Jared make if he has 32 10-inch pieces of wood? Write an equation to help you find the answer. Solve the equation.

Answer _____

Part B Jared sells each frame for $9. He wants to earn $72. How many frames does he need to sell? Explain how you found your answer.

_____
_____
_____
_____

Lesson 18: Two-Step Word Problems

CCLS: 3.OA.8

Part 1: Introduction

Some problems take two steps to solve. That means you have to do two operations to find the answer. The order you do the steps is important.

Write an equation to show a problem.

> Sofia bought 3 packs of pencils. Each pack has 8 pencils in it. She had some pencils already. Now she has 30 pencils. Write an equation to find how many pencils Sofia had already.

Use multiplication to find the total number of pencils Sofia bought: 3×8.

You do not know the number of pencils Sofia already had. Use a letter to stand for this number: p. Sofia has 30 pencils in all. So add.

$$\underbrace{3 \times 8}_{\text{pencils she bought}} + \underbrace{p}_{\text{pencils she had already}} = \underbrace{30}_{\text{total number of pencils}}$$

> **Order of Operations:**
> 1. Parentheses
> 2. Multiply and Divide
> 3. Add and Subtract

> You can use any letter to stand for a number you do not know. Pick a letter that makes sense to you.

Write an equation to solve a problem. Sometimes the operations must be done in the right order. It can make a difference in the answer.

> Brody has $10. Cai has 2 times as much money as Brody. If Cai loans Brody $8, how much will she have left?

First, multiply: $2 \times 10 = 20$.

Next, subtract: $20 - 8 = 12$.

When you combine the steps, the equation looks like this: $2 \times 10 - 8 = 12$.

Think about the order of the operations. If you subtract 8 from 10 first, and then multiplied by 2, the answer is 4. This is not correct. You must multiply before you subtract. You can rewrite the combined number sentence with parentheses. They tell you to multiply first, and then subtract.

$$(2 \times 10) - 8 = 12$$

> Think about what the words mean. *Two times* means to use multiplication. *Loans* means to give away, so you must use subtraction.

> **Parentheses ( )** are grouping symbols. They show what operation must be done first.

146 UNIT 4 Operations and Algebraic Thinking, Part 2

©The Continental Press, Inc. DUPLICATING THIS MATERIAL IS ILLEGAL.

Always think about the answer you found. Does it make sense? You should be on the lookout for mistakes. Sometimes you will see an answer that looks too large or too small. Check your work.

> **Estimate** to check your answer. Round the numbers. Do the operations. Is the answer close to your answer?

Think About It

What is something you do that takes more than one step? Describe what you do. Tell whether the order matters.

_____

_____

 Focused Instruction

Combine addition and subtraction steps to write an equation. Think about word clues.

Cora bought one shirt for $15 and another for $20. She had a coupon that gave her *d* dollars off the total. Write an equation to show how much she paid.

Which word tells the operation to use for the first step?

_____

What is the operation? _____

What is the expression for the first step?

_____

> Think about a coupon. A coupon always takes an amount away.

Which word tells the operation to use for the second step?

_____

What is the operation? _____

Combine the expression for the first step with the second step.

_____

Would the answer be different if the steps were done in a different order? Explain.

_____

_____

Focused Instruction

Some word problems use addition or subtraction and multiplication or division. It is important to think about the order when the operations are not inverses.

Vicki eats 2 pieces of fruit every day of the week. There are 7 days in a week. She has 6 apples. She is on her way to the store to buy more fruit. Vicki wants to buy more fruit to add to the apples she has. She wants to have 2 pieces of fruit every day for a week.

Write the expression to find how many pieces of fruit Vicki needs for

1 week. _____

What operation should you use to find how many more she needs?

_____

Write the expression to combine the first step and the second step.

_____

How many pieces of fruit does Vicki need to buy? _____

What would the answer be for $2 \times 7 - 6$ if the subtraction were done first and

the multiplication second? _____

Suppose you did not know which operation you were supposed to do first. How might you figure out which to do first?

_____

_____

Use parentheses to show which operation should be done first.

_____

> An expression does not have an equal sign.

 **Focused Instruction**   Lesson 18

Use what you know about two-step word problems to solve these problems.

1. Marlon had 50 cents. He found 25 cents on the sidewalk. Then he gave c cents to his sister. Marlon has 65 cents left. Write an equation to show this.

   _____

2. Mario and his sister bought 3 packs of juice boxes. There are 6 boxes in each pack. They split the boxes between them. Write and solve one equation that shows how many juice boxes Mario got.

   _____

Guided Practice

Lesson 18

Solve the following problems.

1. Chase is making a newsletter for his soccer team. On one page, he puts 5 rows of 8 pictures each. On the next page, he puts *p* more pictures. He put 46 pictures in the newsletter in all. Write an equation to show the number of photos Chase put in the newsletter.

   > Look for clues to know what operation to use. *More* usually tells you to add.

   Answer _____

2. Jack earned $15 on Monday. He earned $5 on Tuesday. On Wednesday, he bought lunch for $9.

   > The word *left* is usually a clue that tells you to subtract.

   Part A Write an expression to show the amount of money Jack has left.

   Answer _____

   Part B How much money does Jack have left?

   Answer $_____

3. Heidi saves $8 each week for 6 weeks. At the end of 6 weeks, she spends the money she has saved on a DVD, a book, and a music album. She spends the same amount on each thing.

   > Remember to look for clues in the wording to decide which operation to use.

   Part A Write an equation to find how much Heidi spent on the book.

   Answer _____

   Part B Does it matter which operation is done first? Explain and write equations to support your answer.

   _____
   _____

UNIT 4 Operations and Algebraic Thinking, Part 2

Independent Practice

Lesson 18

Solve the following problems.

1 Dana bought lunch for herself and 3 of her friends. Each lunch cost $8. She left a $5 tip. Which expression shows how much Dana spent?

A $(5 \times 8) + 4$

B $8 \times (5 + 4)$

C $(4 \times 8) + 5$

D $(4 \times 5) + 8$

2 Ziba buys a game that costs $7 and some packs of game cards that cost $4 each. She spent $19 in all. Write an equation you can use to find the number of packs of game cards Ziba bought. Use p for the unknown number.

Answer _____

3 Omar split 18 carrot sticks equally into 3 sandwich bags. Then he ate 2 carrot sticks from one sandwich bag. Write and solve an equation to find how many carrot sticks were left in the bag. Use parentheses to show which operation must be done first. Show your work.

Answer _____

UNIT 4 Operations and Algebraic Thinking, Part 2

Independent Practice — Lesson 18

4 Tyler went to the state spelling bee. His school gave him $50 for travel and $30 a day for his meals. Tyler was given a total of $140. Which of these equations could you use to find the number of days the school paid for his meals? Select the **two** correct answers.

A $(30 + 50) \times n = 140$

B $(30 \times n) + 50 = 140$

C $140 - (30 \times n) = 50$

D $140 \div n = 50 + 30$

E $140 - 50 \times n = 30$

5 Maryanne read the following problem in her math book.

> A third-grade class went on a field trip. There are 24 students in the class. Three students were absent and could not go on the trip. The students that went rode in 3 vans. The same number rode in each van. How many students went in each van?

Part A Maryanne wrote two different expressions she thinks she can use to solve this problem. Find the value of each expression.

$(24 - 3) \div 3 =$ _____

$24 - (3 \div 3) =$ _____

Part B Which answer from Part A seems more reasonable? Explain.

_____

_____

Part C Look at the correct expression. Explain why the parentheses are where they are for that expression.

_____

_____

UNIT 4 Operations and Algebraic Thinking, Part 2

Independent Practice

Lesson 18

6 Eli had a piece of string that was 46 inches long. He cut off a piece that was 15 inches long. Then he cut off another piece that was 12 inches long.

Part A Write two different expressions you could use to find how much string Eli had left.

Expression 1 _____

Expression 2 _____

Part B Explain why you can use both expressions to find the correct answer.

_____
_____
_____
_____

7 A group of 9 students and 1 teacher are going to the museum. Student tickets cost $3 and adult tickets cost $5.

Part A How much does it cost for the group to go to the museum?

Answer $ _____

Part B Explain how you can use estimation to decide if your answer is reasonable.

_____
_____

UNIT 4 Operations and Algebraic Thinking, Part 2

Independent Practice — Lesson 18

8 The prices of some items at a snack stand are shown.

Snack Stand Prices	
Ham Sandwich	$7
Veggie Wrap	$6
Nachos	$4
Cheese Fries	$5
Drinks	$1 each

Part A Ali wants to buy a veggie wrap and some drinks. She has $10. Write an equation Ali can use to find how many drinks she can buy. Use d for the number of drinks.

Answer _____

Part B Kevin has $28. He wants to buy 3 ham sandwiches. Write an equation to find how much Kevin will have left after he buys the sandwiches. Use m for the amount of money Kevin will have left.

Answer _____

Part C Mr. O'Shea bought 2 orders of nachos and 2 orders of cheese fries. Write an equation to find how much Mr. O'Shea spent in all. Use t for the total amount Mr. O'Shea spent.

Answer _____

UNIT 4 REVIEW
Operations and Algebraic Thinking, Part 2

CCLS: 3.OA.3, 8

Solve the following problems.

1. Inez hung 20 paintings. She put them in 5 rows. Write a multiplication equation to show how many paintings Inez hung in each row. Use *n* for the unknown.

   Answer _____

2. A baseball team has 9 players. King School has 36 baseball players. How many teams are there? Use this equation to solve the problem: $36 \div p = 9$.

   Answer _____ teams

3. Manuel placed 28 bottles on a store's shelves. He put an equal number on each of 4 shelves. How many bottles are on each shelf? Use this equation to solve the problem: $4 \times c = 28$.

   A 4

   B 7

   C 20

   D 24

4. Juanita is 10 years old. Her father is 4 times older than her. When Juanita is 30, how old will her father be? Explain how you got your answer.

   _____
   _____
   _____

5 Tony received a gift card worth $25. He bought a book for $8. He bought another book for $11. Write an equation to show how much money Tony had left. Use *n* for the unknown.

Answer _____

6 A pet store puts 8 white mice in each cage. There are a total of 40 mice. Which equations can be used to find *c*, the number of cages of mice? Select the **three** correct answers.

A $8 \times c = 40$

B $8 + 8 + 8 + 8 + c = 40$

C $40 \div c = 8$

D $40 - c = 8$

E $c \div 8 = 40$

F $40 \div 8 = c$

7 A baker wants to bake 60 cookies. He can fit 12 cookies on each baking pan.

Part A Write a multiplication equation and a division equation that could each be used to find out how many trays the baker needs. Use *t* for the unknown.

Multiplication Equation _____

Division Equation _____

Part B Solve one of your equations from Part A for *t*.

Answer _____ trays

8 Jayden bought his mother earrings that cost $14. He also bought her a necklace that cost $18. He had the gifts wrapped for an additional charge of $2. Write an expression to show how much Jayden spent for his mother's gifts.

Answer _____

9 Paige is making bread. Each loaf requires 3 eggs. She has 27 eggs. Can she make 10 loaves of bread? Explain.

_____
_____

10 Trinity is making beaded bracelets for 8 of her friends. She has 47 purple beads and 25 green beads. Each bracelet has the same total number of beads. Write an equation to help you find the total number of beads on each bracelet. Use b for the number you do not know. Solve your equation.

Answer _____

11 Ms. Garcia has some pieces of fabric. She has 3 pieces that are each 6 yards long. She has another piece that is f yards long. She has a total of 30 yards of fabric.

Part A Write an equation to show this situation.

Answer _____

Part B Use your equation for Part A to find how long the last piece of fabric is. Show your work.

Answer _____ yards

UNIT 4 REVIEW Operations and Algebraic Thinking, Part 2

12 Kathy has two apple trees in her yard.

Part A Kathy picks 7 apples from one tree and 9 from the other tree. She uses all the apples to make apple pies. She uses 4 apples to make each pie. How many pies did Kathy make? Show your work.

Answer _____ pies

Part B There are 8 people in Kathy's family. They each eat one piece of pie each day. If the pies are each cut into 6 slices, how many days will the pies last? Show your work.

Answer _____ days

13 Salim has $40. He buys 4 pairs of socks for $7 each. With the money he has left, he buys a sandwich for himself and for each of his 3 sisters. The sandwiches all cost the same amount of money. How much did each sandwich cost? Show your work.

Answer $_____

14 Shen planted tomato plants in his garden. This array shows how they are planted.

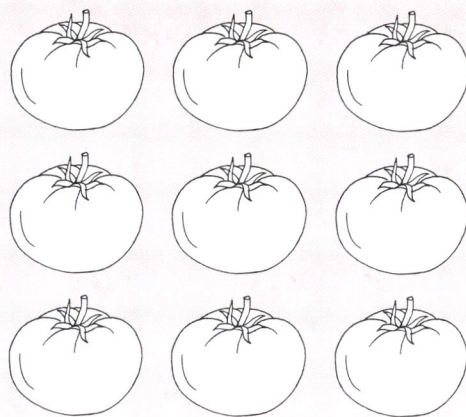

Part A Write and solve an equation to show how many tomato plants Shen planted.

Answer _____

Part B Next year, Shen plans to plant twice as many tomato plants as he did this year. He will plant them at different times so he will have tomatoes all summer. He will plant some in May, some in June, and some in July. He will plant the same number each month. Write and solve an equation to show how many tomato plants Shen will plant each month.

Answer _____

UNIT 5
Number and Operations—Fractions

In Unit 3, you learned how using place-value charts and regrouping help you solve a problem. Now you can use what you know about whole numbers to create and identify fractions.

LESSON 19 Understanding Fractions In this lesson, you will write parts of numbers as fractions using numerators and denominators.

LESSON 20 Fractions on a Number Line In this lesson, you will use number lines to model fractions.

LESSON 21 Equivalent Fractions In this lesson, you will identify fractions that are equal to each other and express whole numbers as fractions.

LESSON 22 Comparing Fractions In this lesson, you will compare fractions by looking at their numerators and denominators.

LESSON 19: Understanding Fractions

CCLS: 3.NF.1

Part 1 Introduction

A whole can be divided into equal parts. A **fraction** compares parts to the whole. The number of parts is called the **numerator**. The total number of parts is called the **denominator**.

$\dfrac{1}{4}$ ← Numerator
← Denominator

The window shown has 4 equal parts. A baseball went through 1 of them.

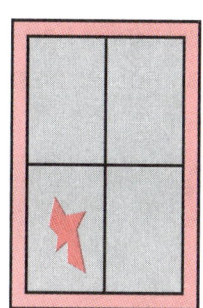

The fraction shows 1 out of 4 parts.

$$\dfrac{1}{4}$$

The rest of the parts are not broken. So 3 out of 4 parts are not broken.

$$\dfrac{3}{4}$$

The parts of a fraction must be equal. So each part is the same size.

Mary cut a pie into 6 slices.

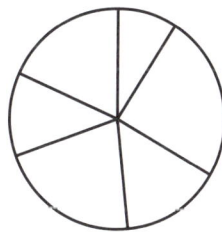 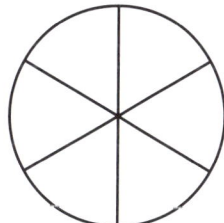

The pie on the left does not show equal parts. The pie on the right does show equal parts.

Mary served 5 slices of the pie on the right. So Mary served $\dfrac{5}{6}$ of the pie.

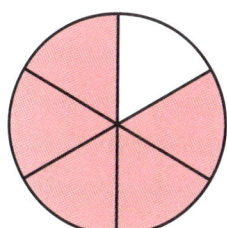

$\dfrac{5}{6}$ ← Number of parts served
← Total number of parts

UNIT 5 Number and Operations—Fractions

Think About It

Is $\frac{1}{2}$ of a small board the same size as $\frac{1}{2}$ of a large board? Explain.

_____

_____

PART 2 Focused Instruction

Fractions can also name parts of a set, such as marbles in a bag or crackers on a plate.

Jamila visited her grandparents for 6 days. On 2 days, Jamila helped her grandmother plant flowers. On 1 day, Jamila helped her grandfather plant vegetables.

Is the number of days Jamila visited her grandparents the part or the whole of a fraction? _____

How many days did Jamila visit her grandparents? _____

Is the number of days Jamila did certain things the part or the whole?

_____

How many days did Jamila help her grandmother plant flowers? _____

Which number goes on top of the fraction, the part or the whole?

_____

Which number goes on the bottom of the fraction, the part or the whole?

_____

What is the fraction of the days that Jamila helped her grandmother?

_____

What is the fraction of the days that Jamila helped her grandfather?

_____

162 UNIT 5 Number and Operations—Fractions

Focused Instruction — Lesson 19

Models can help you understand fractions. Sometimes you may need to draw one to help you.

On a game show, a person gets to choose a door to open. Behind 1 door is a grand prize. Behind 2 doors are smaller prizes. One door does not have a prize behind it.

How many doors are there in all? _____

Is the number of doors the numerator or the denominator of a fraction? _____

Behind how many doors is there a prize? _____

Is the number of doors with a prize the numerator or the denominator? _____

Use the rectangle to draw a model showing the fraction of the doors with a prize behind them.

What fraction of the doors have a prize behind them? _____

> Read the problem carefully. Sometimes you have to find information. It is not always clear.

Use what you know about fractions to write the correct fraction under each model.

1.

2.

3.

_____   _____   _____

UNIT 5 Number and Operations—Fractions

Guided Practice — Lesson 19

Solve the following problems.

1 Some apples are in a basket. Some are beside the basket.

Shade the sections in this model to show the fraction of apples that are beside the basket.

> What is the whole?
> What is the numerator?

2 A fraction of this circle is shaded.

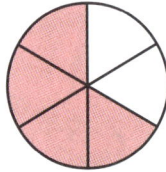

What fraction of the figure is shaded?

Answer _____

> What is the whole?
> What is the part of the whole that the fraction describes?

3 The picture below shows the flag of the country of Austria.

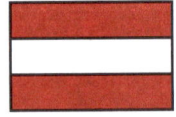

What fraction of Austria's flag is **not** white?

Answer _____

> Which part of the fraction is the numerator?

164 UNIT 5 Number and Operations—Fractions

Independent Practice

Lesson 19

Solve the following problems.

1. In a fraction, what does the numerator show?

   _____

   _____

2. Kai and Aaron ate $\frac{5}{6}$ of a pizza. Explain how you can tell what fraction of the pizza is left.

   _____

   _____

   _____

3. Shade $\frac{3}{8}$ of the figure below.

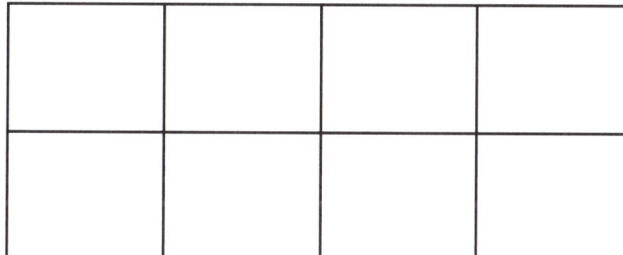

4. Check the boxes above the figures that show $\frac{1}{3}$ shaded.

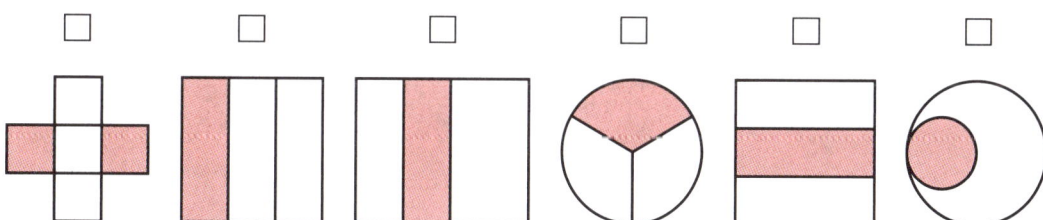

UNIT 5 Number and Operations—Fractions 165

Independent Practice — Lesson 19

5 Look at the fractions in the table. Choose the correct fraction for each model. You may use some fractions more than once.

Fraction	$\frac{1}{2}$	$\frac{5}{8}$	$\frac{5}{6}$	$\frac{6}{8}$
circle (8 parts, 5 shaded)				
triangle (2 parts, 1 shaded)				
rectangle (8 strips, 6 shaded)				
square (2 parts, 1 shaded)				
circle (6 parts, 5 shaded)				

Independent Practice — Lesson 19

6 Lora and Isaiah are planning a vegetable garden. The garden will be in the shape of a rectangle. They want to divide the garden into 6 equal parts.

Part A Lora wants to plant peppers in $\frac{2}{6}$ of the garden. She drew the figure below and shaded the parts for peppers. What mistake did Lora make? Use the rectangle on the right to draw a correct figure.

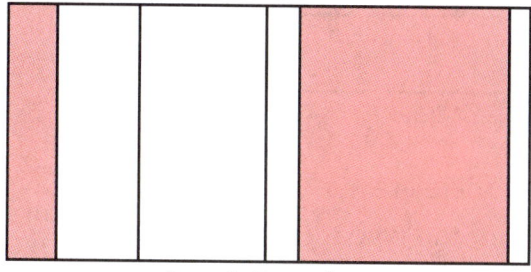
Lora's Drawing

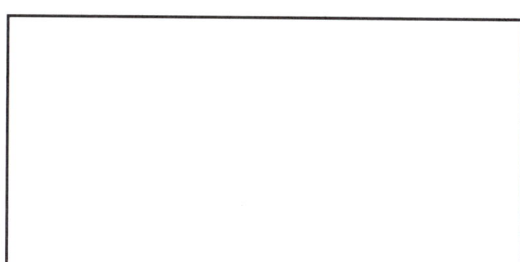

_____

_____

Part B Isaiah also wants to plant peppers in $\frac{2}{6}$ of the garden. He wants to plant cucumbers in $\frac{2}{6}$ of the garden. He also wants to plant corn in $\frac{3}{6}$ of the garden. Can he plant the vegetables this way? Explain.

_____

_____

_____

_____

LESSON 20: Fractions on a Number Line

CCLS: 3.NF.2.a, b

Part 1 Introduction

Use a **number line** to show fractions. Think of the number line as a strip of paper that has been folded to make equal parts.

The left end of the paper is 0. The right end is 1. There are 4 equal parts. The whole is 1 and each part is $\frac{1}{4}$ of the whole. Moving across the number line, the fourths add up: $\frac{1}{4}, \frac{2}{4}, \frac{3}{4}$. The last fraction is $\frac{4}{4}$, which is the same as 1. Notice that the numerators of the fractions change. The denominator, 4, stays the same.

> The **numerator** is the top number in a fraction. The **denominator** is the bottom number.

Look how the number line matches the model above.

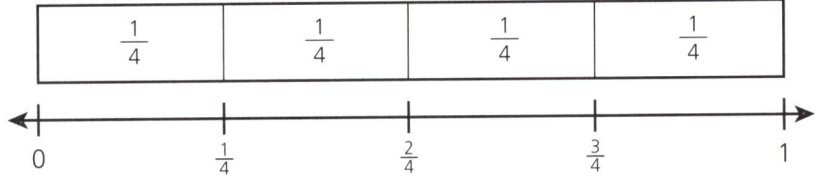

The denominator is the total number of equal parts. For the number line above, the denominator is 4. The number of parts it takes to get to any mark on the number line is the numerator. The numerators shown above are 1, 2, and 3.

> When the numerator and the denominator are the same, the fraction is equal to 1.
> $\frac{4}{4} = 1$

Think of a ruler as a number line. The marks from 0 to 1 inch show equal fractions of an inch. This ruler shows fractions of an inch equal to $\frac{1}{8}$ inch.

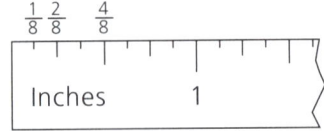

168 UNIT 5 Number and Operations—Fractions

Think About It

Think about the cracks in a sidewalk. How are they like fractions on a number line?

_____

_____

PART 2 Focused Instruction

The space between 0 and 1 on a number line can be divided to show fractions. Use this number line to show fractions.

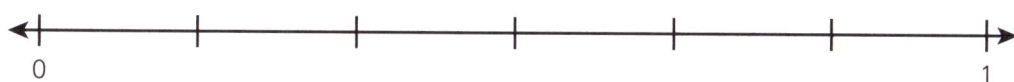

How many spaces separate 0 from 1? _____

How many equal parts make up the whole? _____

What is the denominator of a fraction on this number line? _____

The numerator of a fraction on the number line is given by the number of spaces past _____.

How many marks past 0 is $\frac{1}{6}$? _____ Mark and label $\frac{1}{6}$ on the number line above.

How many marks past 0 is $\frac{4}{6}$? _____ Mark and label $\frac{4}{6}$ on the number line above.

A fraction with a numerator of 1 is called a unit fraction. The fraction $\frac{1}{n}$ is a unit fraction on a number line with n equal spaces. Find and label the unit fraction $\frac{1}{3}$ on the number line below.

What is the denominator of the fraction? _____

How many equal spaces are on the number line? _____

What is the size of each space? _____

Mark and label $\frac{1}{3}$ on the number line above.

Focused Instruction — Lesson 20

The fraction $\frac{a}{n}$ is marked on a number line with *n* equal spaces, and *a* is the number of spaces with a length of $\frac{1}{n}$. Find and label the fraction $\frac{2}{3}$ on the number line below.

Look at the number line above. How many equal parts do you need to make?

_____

What is the numerator in the fraction you want to show? _____

What does this number mean on the number line? _____

Mark and label the fraction $\frac{2}{3}$ where it belongs on the number line.

Use what you know about number lines and fractions to answer these questions.

1. Mark and label $\frac{3}{8}$ on this number line.

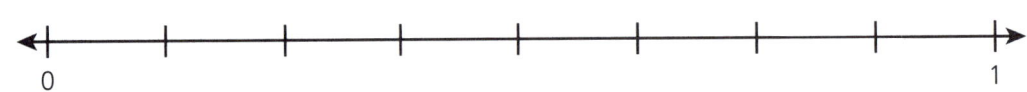

2. How many spaces are on a number line that can represent the fraction $\frac{3}{6}$?

_____

3. Where would the fraction $\frac{8}{8}$ be placed on a number line?

_____

Guided Practice

Lesson 20

Solve the following problems.

1. Draw a number line to show the fraction $\frac{5}{6}$. Mark and label $\frac{5}{6}$ on the number line.

   > What does the denominator show about a number line?

2. Look at the number line below.

   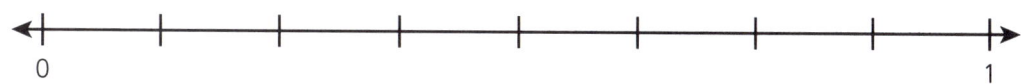

   Part A Is there a mark for $\frac{4}{8}$ on the number line above? If there is, label it. Explain your answer.

   _____

   _____

   > How many spaces are on the line? What does each space equal?

   Part B Is there a mark for $\frac{4}{6}$ on the number line above? If there is, label it. Explain your answer.

   _____

   _____

3. Explain how you would have to change this number line to make it show the fraction $\frac{1}{2}$.

   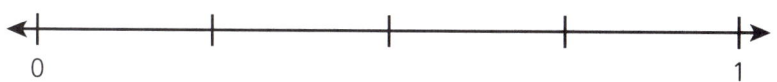

   > What will the spaces between the marks equal after the change?

   _____

   _____

UNIT 5 Number and Operations—Fractions

PART 4 Independent Practice

Lesson 20

Solve the following problems.

1 Where is $\frac{3}{3}$ located on this number line?

- **A** point A
- **B** point B
- **C** point C
- **D** point D

2 What is the missing fraction in the number line?

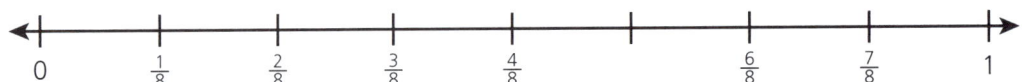

Answer _____

3 Puja drew this number line and labeled $\frac{1}{3}$ on it. Is she correct? Explain why or why not.

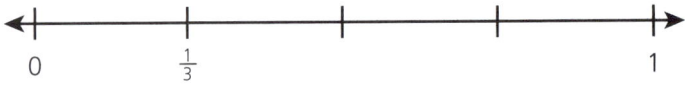

_____
_____

4 Look at the number line below.

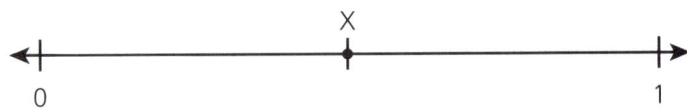

What fraction is marked by point X on this number line?

Answer _____

Independent Practice

Lesson 20

5 Jake walks from the library to the museum along 3rd Avenue. He stops at the post office and at a store. The distances between the streets he crosses are all the same.

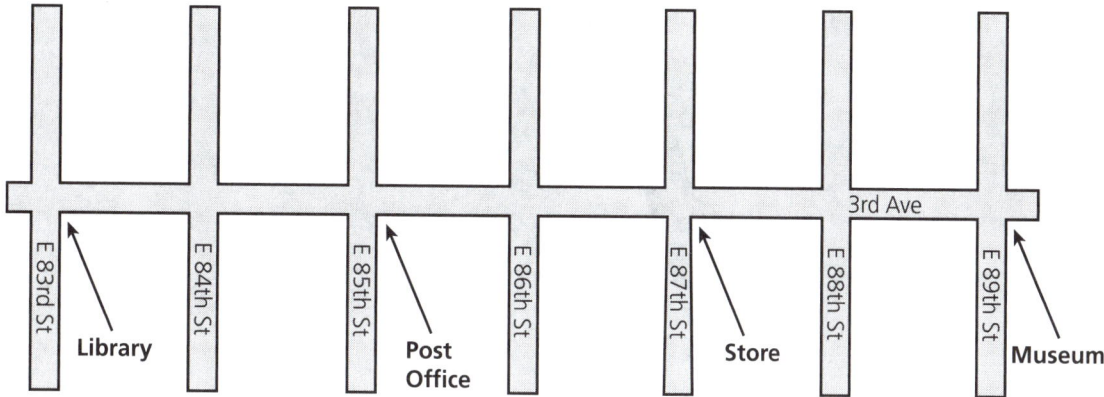

Part A What fraction does the space between two streets represent on this map?

Answer _____

Part B What fraction of the distance from the library to the museum has Jake walked when he reaches the post office?

Answer _____

Part C What fraction of the distance from the library to the museum has Jake walked when he reaches the store?

Answer _____

UNIT 5 Number and Operations—Fractions

Independent Practice

Lesson 20

6 Lillian is standing on this ladder. Think of the ground as 0 on a number line. The steps of the ladder are the same distance apart.

What fraction of the ladder has Lillian climbed?

Answer _____

7 Matt drew a number line to show the distance between his house and his school. His school is 1 mile from his house.

Part A The town library is $\frac{1}{4}$ mile from Matt's house. On the number line, label where the library is.

Part B Every morning, Matt sees a crossing guard $\frac{3}{4}$ mile from his house. Explain how you know where to put a point on the number line to show $\frac{3}{4}$.

_____
_____
_____
_____

LESSON 21: Equivalent Fractions

CCLS: 3.NF.3.a, b, c

Part 1 Introduction

Equivalent fractions are fractions that are the same size. Fraction models can help you find equivalent fractions.

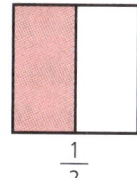 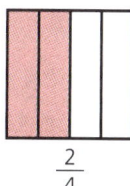 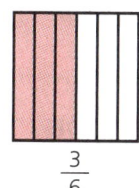 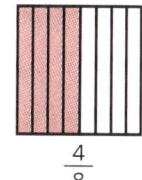

$\frac{1}{2}$ $\frac{2}{4}$ $\frac{3}{6}$ $\frac{4}{8}$

Look at these models. The same amount of each square is shaded. Each model shows a different fraction. The fractions each cover the same part of the square. So the fractions are equivalent.

$$\frac{1}{2} = \frac{2}{4} = \frac{3}{6} = \frac{4}{8}$$

Equivalent fractions fall at the same point on a number line.

The number line shows that $\frac{2}{4}$ is equivalent to $\frac{1}{2}$.

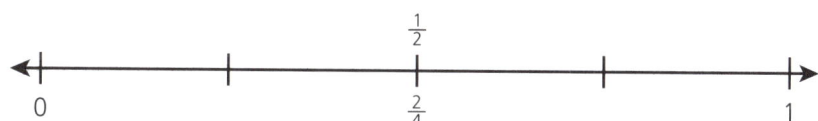

Fractions can also be equivalent to whole numbers. The **identity property** says that any number divided by 1 is still that number. Any number divided by itself is 1. Use this property to understand whole numbers as fractions. Think of a fraction as division.

$$\frac{3}{1} = 3 \div 1, \text{ so } \frac{3}{1} = 3$$

$$\frac{3}{3} = 3 \div 3, \text{ so } \frac{3}{3} = 1$$

> The fraction bar can be used to show division.
> $\frac{1}{2} = 1 \div 2$

UNIT 5 Number and Operations—Fractions

Think About It

Describe a time when you are measuring and you need to find equivalent fractions.

_____

_____

PART 2 Focused Instruction

More than two fractions can be equivalent. The fractions $\frac{3}{4}$ and $\frac{6}{8}$ are equivalent. Use the number line to find another fraction that is equivalent to these two.

Find and label the point for $\frac{3}{4}$ and for $\frac{6}{8}$ on this number line.

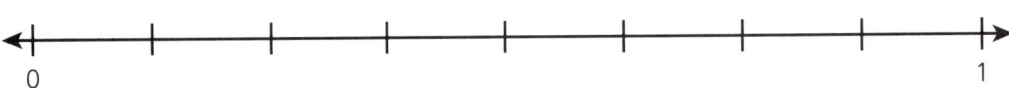

How many spaces does this number line have? _____

How could you change it to show fourths?

_____

Fill in the space to complete this sentence.

The number 8 is _____ times the number 4.

Think about the sentence above. How could you change the number of spaces on the number line to help you find another equivalent fraction?

_____

_____

Change the number line like you described above. Now how many marks after the 0 is the fraction? _____

What is the equivalent fraction? _____

Focused Instruction — Lesson 21

Whole numbers can be written as fractions. Fractions can also be equivalent to whole numbers.

What happens when you divide a whole number by 1?
_____

How can you write 5 ÷ 1 as a fraction? _____

What whole number is this fraction equivalent to? _____

What is true about a fraction with a denominator of 1?
_____

What happens when you divide a whole number by itself? _____

Write 6 ÷ 6 as a fraction. _____

What whole number is this fraction equivalent to? _____

What is always true about a fraction with the same number in the numerator and the denominator? _____

Use what you know about equivalent fractions to write equivalent fractions.

1 $\frac{1}{2} = \frac{\Box}{10}$

2 $\frac{1}{3} = \frac{2}{\Box}$

3 $17 = \frac{\Box}{\Box}$

4 $1 = \frac{9}{\Box}$

UNIT 5 Number and Operations—Fractions

Guided Practice — Lesson 21

Solve the following problems.

1 Use these models to show that the fractions $\frac{2}{3}$ and $\frac{8}{12}$ are equivalent.

> Which part of the fraction shows the total number of spaces in the model?

2 Look at the fraction below.

$$\frac{5}{5}$$

> What does the bar in a fraction mean?

Part A What whole number is this fraction equivalent to?

Answer _____

Part B Use the rectangle below to create a fraction model to prove your answer is correct.

3 There are two equivalent fractions shown on the number line.

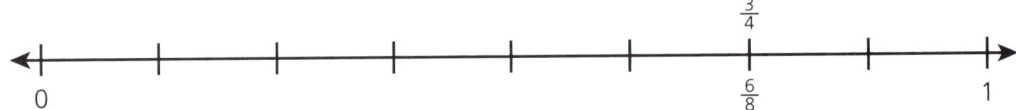

Use the circles below to create fraction models. Show that these fractions are equivalent.

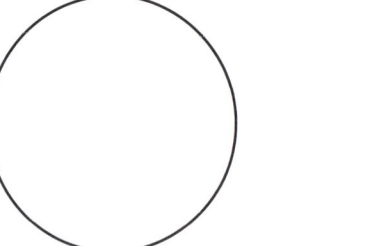
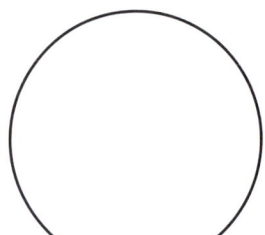

> What does the numerator tell you about the number of shaded sections?

UNIT 5 Number and Operations—Fractions

Independent Practice

Lesson 21

Solve the following problems.

1. The model below shows $\frac{1}{3}$.

   Draw another model that shows an equivalent fraction. What is the equivalent fraction?

   Answer _____

2. Which of the following equations are correct? Select the **three** correct answers.

   A $4 = \frac{4}{1}$

   B $\frac{10}{10} = 0$

   C $9 \div 9 = \frac{9}{9}$

   D $\frac{7}{1} = 8$

   E $\frac{13}{13} = \frac{2}{2}$

3. Write a fraction that is equivalent to $\frac{1}{2}$. Use the models to show you are correct.

   Answer _____

UNIT 5 Number and Operations—Fractions

Independent Practice — Lesson 21

4 Jenna says the fraction $\frac{7}{7}$ is equivalent to 1. Pedro says $\frac{7}{7}$ is equivalent to 7. Who is correct? Explain.

_____

_____

5 Look at the number line below.

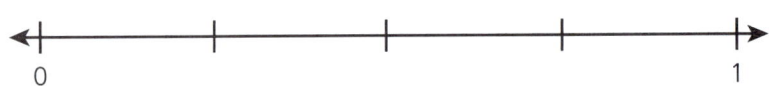

Part A Below each mark on the number line, write a fraction with a denominator of 4.

Part B Above each mark, write an equivalent fraction with a denominator of 8.

6 The rectangle shows a fraction.

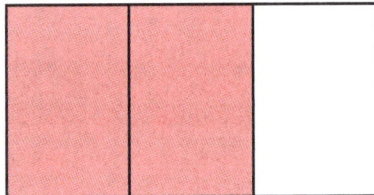

Use the figure below to make a model of an equivalent fraction.

180 UNIT 5 Number and Operations—Fractions

Independent Practice

Lesson 21

7 Will and his sister Leah take turns walking their dog.

Part A Will walked the dog $\frac{2}{4}$ mile on Monday. On Wednesday, Leah walked the dog $\frac{3}{6}$ mile. Will says that he walked farther than Leah. Is he correct? Explain your answer using models or number lines.

_____
_____
_____

Part B The following week, Will walked the dog $\frac{2}{2}$ mile one day. Leah walked the dog $\frac{2}{1}$ miles another day. Who walked the dog farther this week? Explain.

_____
_____
_____
_____

UNIT 5 Number and Operations—Fractions

LESSON 22: Comparing Fractions

CCLS: 3.NF.3.d

Part 1 Introduction

To **compare** fractions means to decide which is larger. You can use symbols to compare fractions. The symbol > means "is greater than." The symbol < means "is less than."

> If two fractions are equal, use the equal sign.
> $\frac{1}{2} = \frac{2}{4}$

When the numerators are the same, the fraction with the smaller denominator is larger.

Compare $\frac{3}{6}$ and $\frac{3}{8}$.

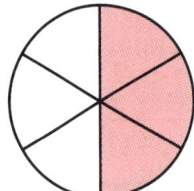 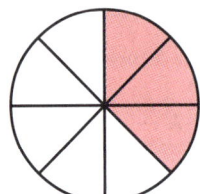

The numerator in both fractions is 3. Look at the denominators. Since 6 is less than 8, $\frac{3}{6} > \frac{3}{8}$.

Look at the models. The fraction model for $\frac{3}{8}$ is divided into more parts. The fraction model for $\frac{3}{6}$ is divided into less parts. The parts of the model for $\frac{3}{8}$ are smaller than the parts for $\frac{3}{6}$.

The 3 larger parts are greater than the 3 smaller parts, so $\frac{3}{6}$ is greater than $\frac{3}{8}$.

$$\frac{3}{6} > \frac{3}{8}$$

When the denominators are the same, the fraction with the larger numerator is greater.

Compare $\frac{4}{6}$ and $\frac{5}{6}$.

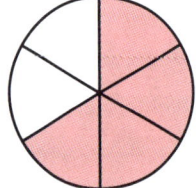 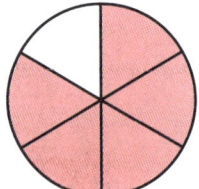

Both models are divided into 6 equal parts. The model for $\frac{4}{6}$ shows that fewer parts are shaded than in the model for $\frac{5}{6}$. So $\frac{4}{6} < \frac{5}{6}$.

UNIT 5 Number and Operations—Fractions

Another way to compare fractions is by using a number line. You can see that $\frac{4}{6}$ is to the left of $\frac{5}{6}$, so $\frac{4}{6}$ must be less than $\frac{5}{6}$.

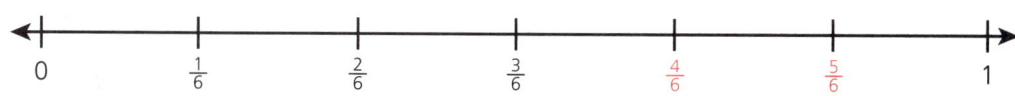

> On a number line, numbers to the left are less than numbers to the right.

Think About It

Suppose you had two pies that were the same size. One pie is cut into 4 pieces and one pie is cut into 8 pieces. Which is bigger: 1 slice from the 4-piece pie or 1 slice from the 8-piece pie? Explain.

_____
_____

PART 2 Focused Instruction

Compare fractions with the same numerator. Decide in which family the boys make up a greater fraction of the children.

Kurt has 2 brothers and 3 sisters. Ivan has 2 brothers and 1 sister.

How many boys are in Kurt's family? _____ Girls? _____

How many children are in Kurt's family? _____

What fraction of the children in Kurt's family are boys? _____

How many boys are in Ivan's family? _____ Girls? _____

How many children are in Ivan's family? _____

What fraction of the children in Ivan's family are boys? _____

Should you use the numerator or the denominator to compare these fractions? How do you compare them?

_____
_____

Use the > symbol to show which fraction is larger. _____

> Remember to count Kurt and Ivan as part of their families.

Focused Instruction

Lesson 22

Check your answer using models. Use the rectangles below.

> When you use models to compare fractions, the models must always be the same size.

Should the rectangles have the same number of sections? _____

Shade the rectangles to model the fractions. Write the fractions to the left of their models.

Compare fractions with the same denominator. Decide which cat's litter had the greater fraction of white kittens.

A cat named Dinah had 6 kittens. Dinah had 3 black and 3 white kittens. A cat named Poofy also had 6 kittens. Poofy had 4 black and 2 white kittens.

Do the fractions have the same denominator or the same numerator?

_____

What is the rule for comparing fractions with the same denominator?

_____

_____

What is the denominator for both fractions? _____

What is the fraction of white kittens Dinah had? _____

What is the fraction of white kittens Poofy had? _____

Use the > symbol to show which is larger. _____

Use what you know about comparing fractions to write the correct symbol in the boxes.

1. $\frac{2}{2}$ ☐ $\frac{2}{8}$ 2. $\frac{2}{3}$ ☐ $\frac{1}{3}$ 3. $\frac{1}{6}$ ☐ $\frac{1}{4}$

184   UNIT 5 Number and Operations—Fractions

Guided Practice

Lesson 22

Solve the following problems.

1 Compare $\frac{5}{8}$ and $\frac{5}{6}$.

Part A Write a symbol to compare the fractions.

$\frac{5}{6}$ ☐ $\frac{5}{8}$

> Check if the numerators or the denominators are the same.

Part B Complete these rectangle models to compare the fractions.

2 Compare $\frac{3}{6}$ and $\frac{4}{6}$.

Part A Write a symbol to compare the fractions.

$\frac{3}{6}$ ☐ $\frac{4}{6}$

> What is the rule for comparing fractions with the same denominator?

Part B Complete the number line to compare the fractions. Circle the fractions being compared.

UNIT 5 Number and Operations—Fractions

Independent Practice

Lesson 22

Solve the following problems.

1 Compare the fractions. Write >, <, or = to complete the number sentence. Draw fraction models to check your answer.

$$\frac{3}{8} \square \frac{3}{4}$$

2 What symbol goes in the box to compare the fractions? Use >, <, or =. Use the number line to show you are correct.

$$\frac{2}{4} \square \frac{3}{4}$$

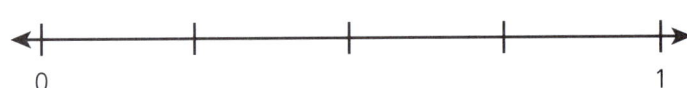

3 Which fraction is greater, $\frac{3}{3}$ or $\frac{2}{3}$? Explain your reasoning.

_____

_____

4 Which of the following number sentences are true? Select the **three** correct answers.

A $\frac{3}{8} > \frac{2}{8}$

B $\frac{4}{4} < \frac{4}{8}$

C $\frac{1}{3} > \frac{2}{3}$

D $\frac{1}{6} < \frac{1}{2}$

E $\frac{2}{4} > \frac{2}{6}$

186 UNIT 5 Number pand Operations—Fractions

Independent Practice

Lesson 22

5 Which pairs of fraction models show correct comparisons? Select the **two** correct answers.

A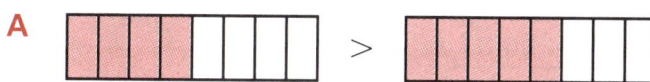

B

C

D

E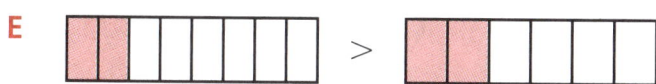

6 Look at the fractions below.

$$\frac{4}{6}, \frac{3}{6}, \frac{3}{8}$$

Part A Put the fractions in order from smallest to largest. Write your answer as one number sentence with < or > symbols between fractions.

Answer _____

Part B Explain how you found your answer.

_____

_____

_____

Independent Practice

Lesson 22

7 Becca and Ronald are comparing the body lengths of different birds for a science project.

BODY LENGTHS OF BIRDS

Bird	Length (feet)
A	$\frac{3}{4}$
B	$\frac{2}{8}$
C	$\frac{2}{6}$
D	$\frac{1}{4}$

Part A Becca drew fraction models to help her compare the lengths of bird B and bird C. She says that the fraction models show that $\frac{2}{8} > \frac{2}{6}$. Explain what Becca did wrong.

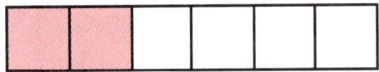

_____
_____
_____

Part B Ronald compares the lengths of bird A and bird D. Which bird has a shorter length? Explain how you know.

_____
_____
_____

188 UNIT 5 Number and Operations—Fractions

UNIT 5 REVIEW
Number and Operations—Fractions

CCLS: 3.NF.1–3

1 Which fraction could go in the box? Select the **two** correct answers.

$$\square > \frac{4}{6}$$

- A $\frac{5}{6}$
- B $\frac{4}{8}$
- C $\frac{2}{6}$
- D $\frac{1}{6}$
- E $\frac{4}{4}$
- F $\frac{3}{6}$

2 Where is $\frac{5}{8}$ located on this number line?

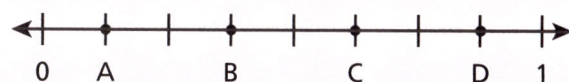

- A point A
- B point B
- C point C
- D point D

3. Which of the following comparisons are correct? Select the **three** correct answers.

A $\frac{3}{4} > \frac{4}{4}$

B $\frac{1}{3} > \frac{1}{8}$

C $\frac{2}{8} > \frac{2}{4}$

D $\frac{2}{6} < \frac{5}{6}$

E $\frac{9}{9} < \frac{9}{1}$

4. Decide if each fraction in the table is greater than, less than, or equivalent to $\frac{2}{4}$. Mark the correct place in the table.

Fraction	Greater than $\frac{2}{4}$	Less than $\frac{2}{4}$	Equivalent to $\frac{2}{4}$
$\frac{2}{8}$			
$\frac{4}{4}$			
$\frac{1}{2}$			
$\frac{2}{2}$			
$\frac{3}{6}$			
$\frac{1}{4}$			
$\frac{2}{6}$			
$\frac{2}{3}$			

5. Naomi used a number line to locate $\frac{3}{6}$. Is she correct? Explain.

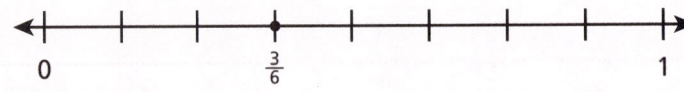

6   Emily and Maneesh are eating sandwiches. Emily ate 2 pieces of her sandwich.

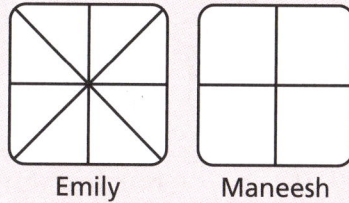

Emily   Maneesh

Maneesh ate an equivalent fraction of his sandwich as Emily. How many pieces of his sandwich did Maneesh eat? Explain.

_____

_____

7   Which pairs of models correctly show equivalent fractions? Select the **four** correct answers.

A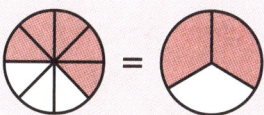

B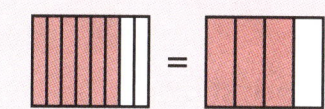

C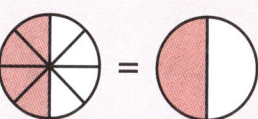

D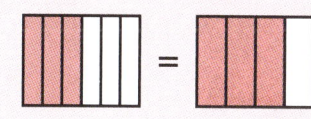

E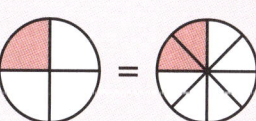

F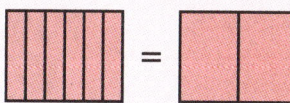

8 Look at the rectangle below.

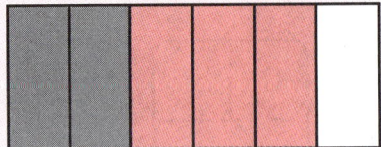

Part A What fraction is shaded gray? What fraction is shaded red?

Gray _____

Red _____

Part B Compare the two fractions using a < or > sign.

Answer _____

Part C Write an equivalent fraction for each of the fractions.

Gray _____

Red _____

9 Three different fractions are shown below. They are each shown in a different way.

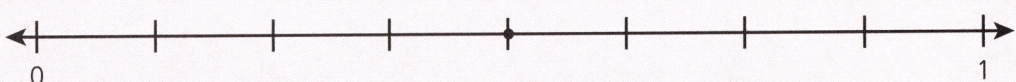

$\frac{5}{8}$

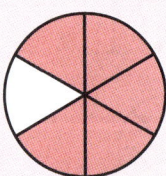

Write the three fractions in order from smallest to largest and separated by < symbols.

Answer _____

192 UNIT 5 REVIEW Number and Operations—Fractions

10 Toni and Preston are reading the same book for Reading class.

Part A Toni has read $\frac{3}{8}$ of the book. Preston has read $\frac{2}{8}$ of the book. Who has read more of the book? Explain.

_____
_____
_____

Part B A few days later, Toni has finished $\frac{3}{3}$ of the book. Preston has finished $\frac{4}{4}$ of the book. Preston says that they have read the same amount. Is he correct? Explain.

_____
_____
_____
_____

11 Ginnie recorded the eye color of everyone in her family.

Dad	Mom	Sam	Ginnie	Kate	Logan
blue	brown	brown	brown	blue	green

Part A What fraction of the family has brown eyes?

Answer _____

Part B In Zena's family, the same fraction of the family has brown eyes as in Ginnie's family. There are 4 people in Zena's family. Write a fraction that shows the fraction of Zena's family that has brown eyes. Explain how you found your answer.

_____
_____
_____

12 Hannah's garden is divided into equal sections. She plants different things in her garden.

corn	carrots	lettuce	peas
strawberries	raspberries	blueberries	sunflowers

Part A Find the fraction of the garden that has each type of plant.

Vegetables _____

Fruit _____

Flowers _____

Part B Plot and label a point on the number line for each type of plant.

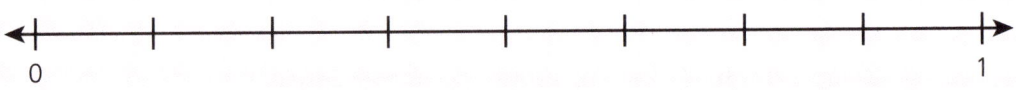

UNIT 6
Measurement and Data

In grade 2, you learned how to measure length and read picture graphs and bar graphs. You also learned how to tell time. Now you can use what you know about measurement and time to analyze data and measure time intervals, mass, length, area, and perimeter.

LESSON 23 Time In this lesson, you will learn how to tell time using the position of the hands on a clock.

LESSON 24 Solving Problems with Time In this lesson, you will measure time intervals by using number lines and by using addition and subtraction.

LESSON 25 Liquid Volume In this lesson, you will measure the volume of liquids in containers.

LESSON 26 Mass In this lesson, you will measure mass using grams and kilograms as units of measurement.

LESSON 27 Picture Graphs In this lesson, you will solve problems by creating and reading picture graphs and tally charts.

LESSON 28 Bar Graphs In this lesson, you will solve problems by creating and using bar graphs.

LESSON 29 Measurement Data on Line Plots In this lesson, you will measure length and record your measurements using line plots.

LESSON 30 Understanding Area In this lesson, you will solve for the area of figures by counting unit squares.

LESSON 31 Multiplying to Find Area In this lesson, you will solve for the area of rectangles using multiplication and tiling.

LESSON 32 Adding to Find Area In this lesson, you will solve for the area of rectangles by using the distributive property, separating irregular figures into rectangles, and tiling.

LESSON 33 Perimeter and Area In this lesson, you will find the area and perimeter of rectangles and find rectangles with the same areas or the same perimeters.

Time

CCLS: 3.MD.1

Part 1 Introduction

Use a **clock** to tell the time. On a clock face, the short hand, which is called the **hour hand,** shows the **hour.** When the hour hand moves from one number to the next, one hour has passed. The long hand, which is called the **minute hand,** shows the **minutes.** When the minute hand moves from one tick mark to the next, one minute has passed.

The clock below shows the time Edan woke up this morning.

> An easy way to remember the clock hands is that the shorter hand of the clock is for the shorter word *hour*. The long hand of the clock is for the longer word *minutes*.

First, look at the hour hand. The hour hand is a little past the 7. So the hour is 7.

> 1 hour = 60 minutes
>
> A.M. = hours from midnight to noon, 9:00 A.M. is 9 o'clock in the morning.
>
> P.M. = hours from noon to midnight, 9:00 P.M. is 9 o'clock in the evening.

Next, look at the minute hand. Since the minute hand is past the 12, the time is after 7:00. The minute hand is 4 tick marks past the 2. Each labeled number on a clock is at a 5-minute tick mark. So, to find the minutes, start at the 12. Going clockwise (to the right), skip count by 5s until you get to the clock's number 2: 5, 10. Then, count 4 tick marks, or minutes, past 10: 11, 12, 13, 14. It is 14 minutes after 7:00.

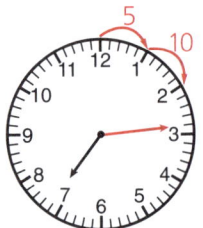

> Time is expressed with a colon separating the hour from the minutes.

Edan woke up this morning at 14 minutes after 7. Write the time as 7:14 A.M.

196 UNIT 6 **Measurement and Data**

Think About It

Think about the time you usually come home from school. What does the clock look like? Where is the short hand and where is the long hand? Explain what time it is using the clock hands.

_____

_____

 Focused Instruction

The hour hand moves between two numbers each hour. It does not always point directly at a number. Sometimes it is between two numbers.

Bret left for soccer practice at the time shown on the clock.

Remember, each skip-counted number represents 5 minutes, and each tick mark is 1 minute.

What does a short hand on a clock show? _____

Where is the short hand on the clock?

_____

What does a long hand on a clock show? _____

Where is the long hand on the clock?

_____

If you skip count by 5s from the number 12 to get to the long hand, how many times will you count? _____

Multiply the number of times you skip counted by 5. _____

The minute hand does not point directly to a number. How many tick marks after the number is the minute hand at? _____

How many more minutes do the extra tick marks represent? _____

**Focused Instruction**   Lesson 23

How many total minutes are there? _____

What is the time on this clock? _____

Time can be written in different ways. You can use a colon. You can also write time by telling the number of minutes before or after an hour.

Freddy's favorite TV show comes on every afternoon at the time shown at the right.

How many hours and minutes are shown on the clock?

_____ hours _____ minutes

Is this time A.M. or P.M.? _____

What keyword tells you if the time is A.M. or P.M.?

_____

Write the time using a colon. _____

Write the time by telling the number of minutes **past** the hour.

_____

Write the time by telling the number of minutes **before** the next hour.

_____

> To write other versions of the time, think about the number of hours and the number of minutes.

Use what you know about time to show the time by drawing the hands on each clock.

1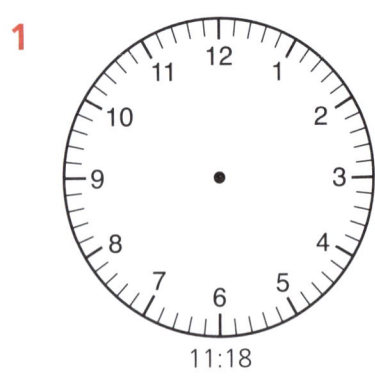
11:18

2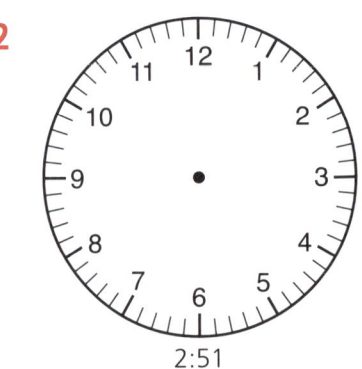
2:51

198   **UNIT 6** Measurement and Data

Guided Practice

Solve the following problems.

1. What does 8:41 P.M. look like on a clock?

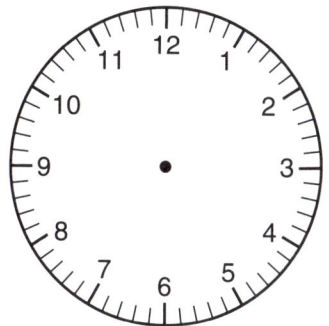

> The number to the left of the colon gives the hour.

2. One evening, Evan and Marc met each other at the time shown below to see a movie.

Part A Write the time that Evan and Marc met in two ways.

Answer _____

Part B They got out of the movie theater at 9:39 P.M. On the clock face below, show the time that Evan and Marc got out of the theater.

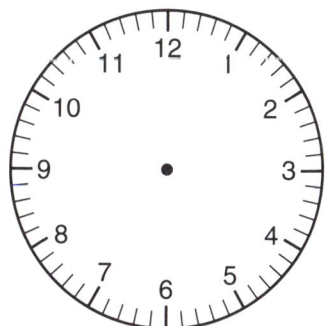

> Use skip counting by 5s to help you draw the minute hand in the correct place.

Independent Practice

Lesson 23

Solve the following problems.

1. Which clock shows 11:11?

   A

   B

   C

   D

2. Sharon left her sister's house at 2:29 P.M. Does the clock below show this time? Explain why or why not.

   _____
   _____
   _____

Independent Practice

Lesson 23

3 An airplane left the airport at the time shown on this clock.

What time did the airplane leave?

A 4:37

B 7:22

C 7:42

D 8:22

4 Kayla started studying for her math test at 6:15 P.M.

Part A What is another way of writing this time?

Answer _____

Part B Draw this time on the clock.

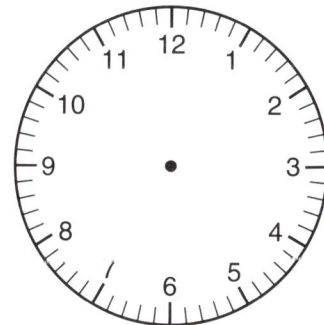

Independent Practice

Lesson 23

5 Jane finished her bike ride at 57 minutes past 2. Draw the time on the clock face below.

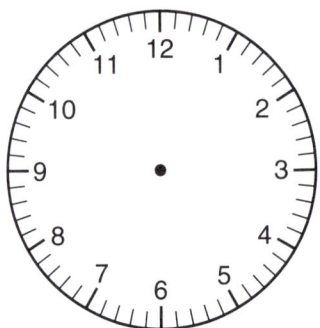

6 Doug says that this clock shows 8:43. Is he correct? Explain why or why not.

_____
_____
_____

Lesson 24

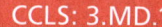

Solving Problems with Time

Part 1 Introduction

Solve problems using time to find how much time has gone past, or the **elapsed time.** You can also find the time something started or ended.

> **Elapsed time** is also called a **time interval.**

Yuri left for school at 8:15 A.M. It took him 25 minutes to get to school.

Add to find what time Yuri got to school.

```
  8:15  ← Start Time
 +0:25  ← Time Interval
  8:40  ← End Time
```

Yuri arrived at school at 8:40 A.M.

Yuri left his friend's house at 4:12 P.M. and arrived home at 4:58 P.M.

```
  4:58  ← End Time
 −4:12  ← Start Time
  0:46  ← Time Interval
```

It took Yuri 46 minutes to get home from his friend's house.

> Remember that the times between midnight and noon are A.M. times. The times between noon and midnight are P.M.

> You will also use subtraction to find the start time when you know the end time and the elapsed time.

A number line can help you solve problems with time.

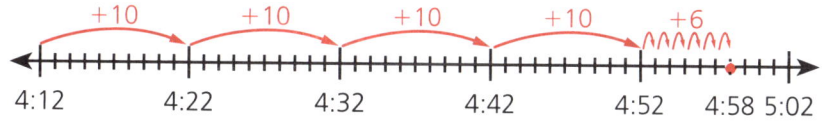

Think About It

What time does your school start in the morning? What time do you leave your house to go to school? Find the amount of time that goes by from the time you leave your house to the time your school starts. Why is this important to know?

_____

_____

_____

_____

UNIT 6 Measurement and Data   **203**

 **Focused Instruction**   Lesson 24

Use subtraction to find the time something started when you know the time it ended and how much time passed. Use addition to find the end time when you know the time something started and how much time passed.

Astrid finished her homework at 6:55 P.M. She had worked on her homework for 40 minutes.

What time did Astrid finish? _____

How much time had elapsed since she started? _____

Is the time she started before 6:55 or after 6:55? _____

Do you need to use subtraction or addition to find the time Astrid started her homework? _____

Use the correct operation to find the time she started her homework.

What time did Astrid start her homework? _____

As soon as she finished her homework, Astrid practiced piano for 25 minutes.

What time did Astrid start practicing her piano? _____

How long did she spend practicing? _____

What operation should you use to find the time Astrid finished practicing piano? _____

Use the correct operation to find the time she finished practicing piano.

> When you add or subtract across an hour, you may need to regroup 60 minutes as 1 hour or 1 hour as 60 minutes.

What time did Astrid finish practicing piano? _____

Focused Instruction — Lesson 24

Time lines, or number lines, can also help you solve problems with time.

Troy and Aamir met at the playground at 10:10 A.M. They played for 65 minutes.

Use a number line to find the time that the boys finished playing.

What time did the boys start playing? _____

Where is this time on the number line? _____

The number line shows marks for 10 minutes. Write the actual time under each mark on the number line above.

> There are 60 minutes in an hour.

What time did the boys finish playing? _____

Use what you know about time to fill in this table.

Start Time	End Time	Elapsed Time
11:14		33 minutes
	9:02	1 hour 2 minutes
5:27	6:08	

UNIT 6 Measurement and Data

Guided Practice

Lesson 24

Solve the following problems.

1 Bryan worked on a science project from 10:07 A.M. to 10:49 A.M. How many minutes did he work on his project?

Should you add or subtract to find the elapsed time?

Answer _____ minutes

2 Baz got to the library at 7:45 A.M. He read the sign on the library. How long will he have to wait before the library opens?

PUBLIC LIBRARY
Daily Hours
9 A.M.–6 P.M.

Answer _____

3 The elementary music program began at 7:00 P.M.

Part A The first half of the program ended at 7:46. There was a 12-minute break before the second half started. What time did the second half start? Show your work.

Answer _____

Part B The second half of the program lasted 38 minutes. How long was the entire elementary music program? Show your work.

Remember to include the break as part of the program.

Answer _____

UNIT 6 Measurement and Data

Independent Practice — Lesson 24

Solve the following problems.

1 Lexi left to go to the park at 3:15 P.M. She got to the park at 3:42 P.M. How long did it take Lexi to get to the park?

Answer _____ minutes

2 Paul finished cleaning his room at 4:50 P.M. after working on it for 43 minutes. What time did Paul start cleaning his room?

A   4:17 P.M.

B   4:53 P.M.

C   4:43 P.M.

D   4:07 P.M.

3 Colby began making lunch at the time shown on the left. He finished at the time shown on the right.

Start   End

How long did it take Colby to make lunch? Show your work.

Answer _____ minutes

UNIT 6 Measurement and Data

Independent Practice

Lesson 24

4 Deb started exercising at 11:11 A.M. She exercised for 39 minutes. Use the time line to find what time Deb finished exercising.

Start
11:11

Answer _____

5 Dion started reading a book at 10:10 A.M. He stopped reading at 12:00 noon. How long did Dion read?

   A 50 minutes

   B 1 hour 40 minutes

   C 1 hour 50 minutes

   D 2 hours 10 minutes

6 Jerome flew from Dallas, Texas, to Chicago, Illinois. He left Dallas at 1:45 P.M. and arrived in Chicago at 4:05 P.M. Rachel also flew from Dallas to Chicago. She left Dallas at 9:00 A.M. and arrived in Chicago at 11:35 A.M. Whose flight took the longer amount of time? Explain.

_____

_____

_____

7 Norah has homework in different subjects. Complete the table to show the start time, end time, or elapsed time for each subject's homework.

Subject	Start Time	End Time	Elapsed Time
Math	3:55	4:13	
Reading		4:45	30 minutes
Spelling	4:47		24 minutes
Science	5:14	5:22	

UNIT 6 Measurement and Data

Independent Practice

8 Liam is taking a train to visit his grandparents. The train schedule below shows the trains that leave from Liam's town. All the trains stop in the town where his grandparents live.

TRAIN SCHEDULE

Train Number	Departs
245	7:30 A.M.
119	8:45 A.M.
21	9:45 A.M.
1010	12:15 P.M.

Part A Liam wants to get to his grandparents' town close to 10:30 A.M. The trip takes 1 hour 30 minutes. What train should Liam take?

Answer _____

Part B It takes Liam 1 hour 20 minutes to get ready and get to the train. If he starts getting ready at 7:15 A.M., will he be able to catch the 8:45 A.M. train? Explain.

_____
_____
_____

LESSON 25: Liquid Volume

CCLS: 3.MD.2

PART 1 Introduction

Capacity is the amount that a container can hold. Capacity is also the amount of space taken up by a liquid. You can measure the amount of space taken up by a liquid. This is called **volume.** When you measure volume in metric units, you use **liters.**

A large water bottle holds about 1 liter of liquid.

liter (L)

This container can hold 10 liters.

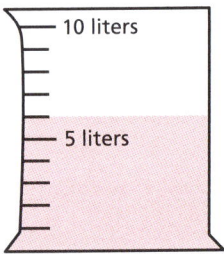

The scale marks show each liter. There are 6 liters in the container.

Use L to stand for *liters.*

Use operations to solve problems with liters.

Jace filled a 5-liter container with sports drink. He gave the drink to runners at a race. He filled the container 4 times in all. The runners drank all the sports drink. How many liters did Jace give to the runners?

Decide what operation to use. The words *4 times* tell you to multiply.

Write a number sentence to solve the problem.

$$5 \times 4 = 20$$

Jace gave 20 liters of sports drink to the runners.

To **estimate** a liquid volume, decide about how much something holds. Think about something familiar. A water bottle holds about 1 liter. You can think of a water bottle to help you estimate.

Think About It

Think of a situation where you would need to measure an exact volume of liquid. Think of a situation where you might estimate the volume.

_____

_____

_____

_____

PART 2 Focused Instruction

Pictures can help you solve a problem involving volume. You must be able to read the scale on the picture to see how much liquid the picture shows.

Anita brought 4 liters of lemonade to the party. Gilberto brought 3 liters of lemonade. How many liters did Anita and Gilberto bring in all?

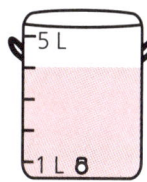

How many liters are in this container? _____

Whose lemonade is shown?

_____

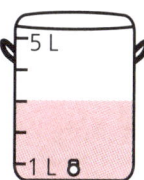

How many liters are in this container? _____

Whose lemonade is shown?

_____

Use the scale marks to figure out how many liters are in the container.

What operation should you use to find the answer? _____

Write a number sentence to help you solve the problem.

_____

How many liters did Anita and Gilberto bring in all? _____

UNIT 6 Measurement and Data

Decide what operation you need to use to solve this problem. Look for key words.

Lee's class had a tub with 15 liters of water in it. The class watered the garden. There were 7 liters left in the tub. How many liters did the class use?

How many liters were in the container to start? _____

How many liters were in the container when the class finished? _____

What operation must you use to solve the problem? _____

How many liters of water did the class use? _____

Use what you know about liquid volume to answer these questions.

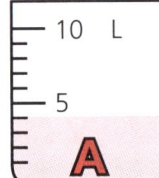 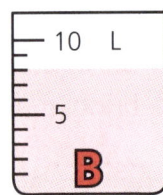 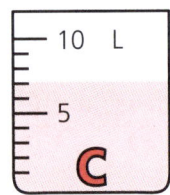

1 How many liters are in containers A and B? _____

2 How many more liters are in container C than container A? _____

3 If there are 6 other containers with the same amount of liquid as container B, how many liters are there in the 7 containers in all? _____

Guided Practice

Solve the following problems.

1 Kirk uses 3 liters of milk to make a large pot of hot chocolate. How many liters of milk would he use to fill 4 of these pots? Explain.

_____

_____

_____

Think about what operation to use to solve the problem.

2 Which item holds closest to 100 liters, a bathtub or a lemonade pitcher?

Is 100 liters a big volume or a small volume?

Answer _____

3 Neve uses 32 liters of water to wash her car. Then she uses 14 liters of water to wash her dog. How much water did Neve use in all?

What is the problem asking you to do? This gives a hint about which operation to use.

Answer _____ liters

Part 4 Independent Practice

Lesson 25

Solve the following problems.

1 Katya has to put 54 liters of water equally into 6 containers. How much water should she put in each container?

  A 8 liters

  B 9 liters

  C 54 liters

  D 60 liters

2 A bottle holds 3 liters of juice. How many liters can 5 of these bottles hold? Write and solve a number sentence to show the answer.

  Answer _____

3 Which of the following things most likely holds more than 1,000 liters of water? Select the **three** correct answers.

  A kitchen sink

  B baby bottle

  C pond

  D fire engine tanker

  E bucket

  F swimming pool

  G washing machine

UNIT 6 Measurement and Data

Independent Practice

4 Mike used 13 liters of water washing breakfast dishes. He used 16 liters of water washing lunch dishes. How many liters did Mike use in all?

A 3 L

B 16 L

C 29 L

D 39 L

5 A fruit punch recipe calls for 2 liters of pineapple juice, 1 liter of cranberry juice, and 3 liters of fruit juice.

Part A Alison poured the juices into this container. Draw a line to show the amount of juice in this container.

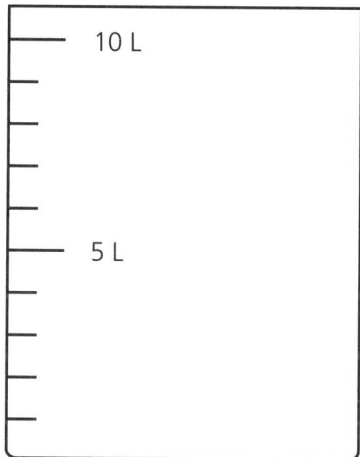

Part B Alison decides to make 4 batches of this recipe for a movie night at the school. How many liters of each type of juice must Alison buy?

Pineapple Juice _____ liters

Cranberry Juice _____ liters

Fruit Juice _____ liters

Part C How many liters of fruit punch will Alison make in all?

Answer _____ liters

Part 4 Independent Practice — Lesson 25

6 Which holds closer to 3 liters, a puddle or a lake?

Answer _____

7 Gene put a small fountain in his backyard.

Part A Gene put 18 liters of water in the fountain. On the container below, draw a line to show the amount of water.

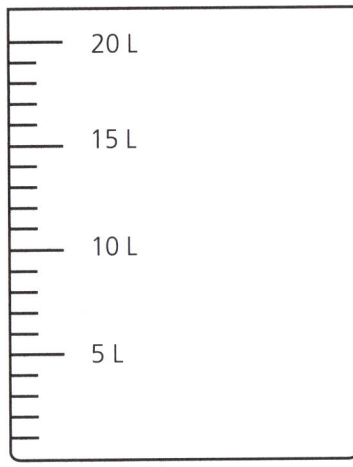

Part B Gene put the pump in his fountain. It pumps 8 liters of water in 1 minute. How many minutes will it take to pump 56 liters of water? Explain how you found your answer.

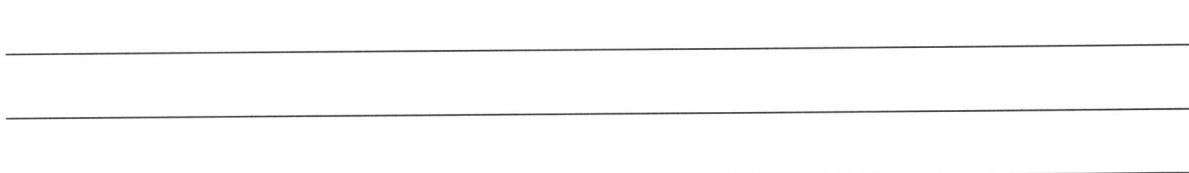

LESSON 26: Mass

CCLS: 3.MD.2

PART 1 Introduction

Mass is how heavy something is. There are two metric units for measuring mass. A **gram** is about the mass of a paper clip. A **kilogram** is about the mass of a baseball bat. The prefix *kilo-* means "thousand." A kilogram is equal to 1,000 grams.

> Most countries in the world use the metric system. This system is based on powers of 10.

Before you measure an object, check if the scale you are using measures grams or kilograms.

Use grams to measure the mass of light objects.	Use kilograms to measure the mass of heavy objects.
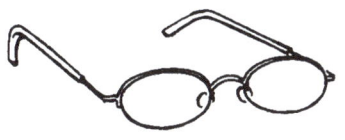	

> Use g to stand for *grams*. Use kg to stand for *kilograms*.

You can solve problems with mass by using all four operations. You can add, subtract, multiply, or divide with grams and kilograms.

A pile of picture books weighs 15 kilograms. A pile of dictionaries weighs 23 kilograms. How many more kilograms do the dictionaries weigh than the picture books?

Decide what operation to use. The words *how many more* are a clue to subtract.

Write a number sentence to solve the problem: 23 − 15 = 8.

The dictionaries weigh 8 kilograms more than the picture books.

UNIT 6 Measurement and Data

Think About It

Think about how you would weigh yourself in metric units. Would you use grams or kilograms? Why?

_____
_____
_____
_____

PART 2 Focused Instruction

Use a picture or model to help you solve problems with mass. Read the scale carefully. Be sure you understand what it shows.

Rico buys an MP3 player. The picture shows the mass of the MP3 player. What is the mass of 2 of these MP3 players?

Which unit does the scale show? _____

What do the numbered tick marks on the scale show? _____

What do the unnumbered tick marks on the scale show? _____

How much does Rico's MP3 player weigh? _____

Write a number sentence that shows how much 2 MP3 players weigh.

_____

Focused Instruction — Lesson 26

Estimate mass by rounding numbers. Use estimation to find the answer to the question.

The mass of 4 crackers is 52 grams. About how many crackers would Lena need if she wanted 150 grams of crackers?

What is the exact mass of the 4 crackers? _____

What is the mass rounded to the nearest ten? _____

Estimate the mass of 8 crackers. _____

Estimate the mass of 12 crackers. _____

What number did you count by to find the answer? _____

How could you find the answer to this problem using multiplication?

_____

_____

> When you find an estimate, first round the numbers with which you are working.

Use what you know about mass to answer these questions.

1. If 8 pens have a mass of 40 grams, what is the mass of 1 pen?

   _____

2. One bag of potatoes has a mass of 5 kilograms. What would the mass of 7 bags of potatoes be? _____

3. The Carson family buys some pumpkins. The pumpkins are 9 kilograms, 15 kilograms, 12 kilograms, and 28 kilograms. What is the total mass of the Carson family's pumpkins? _____

Guided Practice — Lesson 26

Solve the following problems.

1 Dara's dog has a mass of 15 kilograms. Akio's dog has a mass of 23 kilograms. What is the difference in the masses of the two dogs? Show your work.

> Think about what operation you should use to solve the problem.

Answer _____ kilograms

2 A pair of earbuds had a mass of 12 grams. The packaging for the earbuds had a mass of 19 grams.

Part A What was the total mass of the earbuds and the packaging? Show your work.

> What is the problem asking you to do? This gives a hint about what operation to use.

Answer _____ grams

Part B A store has 6 packages of these earbuds on a shelf. What is the total mass of these 6 earbud packages? Show your work.

Answer _____ grams

UNIT 6 Measurement and Data

Solve the following problems.

1. A bag of sugar has a mass of 4 kg. What would the mass of 10 bags of sugar be?

   A 10 kg
   B 14 kg
   C 40 kg
   D 100 kg

2. There are 76 grams of cookies in a snack pack. How many grams of cookies are in 4 snack packs? Explain how you found your answer.

   _____
   _____
   _____

3. Which of the following is the best estimate for the mass of a squirrel?

   A 400 kilograms
   B 40 kilograms
   C 4 grams
   D 400 grams

4. Dashal has a load of boxes that weighs 81 kilograms. If he divides the boxes into 9 equal piles, how much will each pile weigh? Show your work.

   Answer _____ kilograms

UNIT 6 Measurement and Data

Independent Practice

5 Aida is making cornbread with the recipe below. The recipe makes 1 loaf of bread.

Cornbread

120 g flour
170 g cornmeal
48 g sugar
20 g baking powder
2 eggs
salt (to taste)

Part A Aida wants to make 2 loaves of cornbread. She estimates that she will need 100 grams of sugar. Is her estimate correct? Explain why or why not.

_____
_____
_____

Part B Aida realizes that she only has 40 grams of cornmeal. How much more cornmeal does she need in order to make 2 loaves of bread? Explain.

_____
_____
_____
_____

Independent Practice

6. Check the box in the table to show the best estimate for the mass of each object.

Object	1 gram	1 kilogram	10 kilograms
bicycle			
rubber band			
loaf of bread			
shoelace			

LESSON 27: Picture Graphs

CCLS: 3.MD.3

Part 1 Introduction

A **picture graph** is a graph that displays a data set using **symbols**. A **tally chart** can be used to collect and display **data**. A tally chart shows one **tally mark** for one piece of data.

> Data is information.

In a picture graph, a symbol stands for a certain number of data in the set. Look at the two ways to display data below. The tally chart helps you to make the picture graph.

A tally chart shows one tally mark for each vote students cast for their favorite sport.

FAVORITE SPORT

Sport	Number of Votes
Baseball	ⅢⅠ ⅢⅠ ⅢⅠ ⅢⅠ
Soccer	ⅢⅠ ⅢⅠ ⅢⅠ ⅢⅠ ⅢⅠ ⅢⅠ ⅢⅠ
Lacrosse	ⅢⅠ ⅢⅠ ⅢⅠ ⅢⅠ ⅢⅠ
Football	ⅢⅠ ⅢⅠ ⅢⅠ ⅢⅠ ⅢⅠ ⅢⅠ

A picture graph shows one picture for every 5 votes.

FAVORITE SPORT

Sport	Number of Votes
Baseball	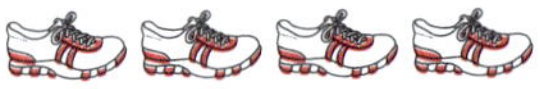 👟 👟 👟 👟
Soccer	 👟 👟 👟 👟 👟 👟 👟
Lacrosse	 👟 👟 👟 👟 👟
Football	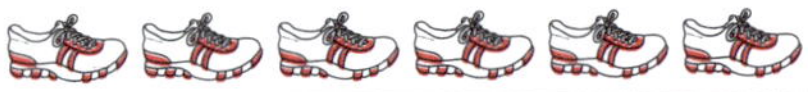 👟 👟 👟 👟 👟 👟

Key: 👟 = 5 votes

Read a picture graph's key carefully.

To find the number of votes for each sport, multiply the number of symbols by the number of votes each symbol stands for.

4 sneakers × 5 votes = 20 votes for baseball
7 sneakers × 5 votes = 35 votes for soccer

Use the picture graph to solve problems. Think about what operation to use to solve the problem.

How many more students voted for soccer than for baseball?

There were 35 votes for soccer. There were 20 votes for baseball.
To find how many more, subtract: 35 − 20 = 15.
So, 15 more people voted for soccer than baseball.

UNIT 6 Measurement and Data

Think About It

When might you use a picture graph to display data?

_____

_____

 Focused Instruction

Read the data in the tally chart. Then use the data from the tally chart to make a picture graph.

MEALS COOKED

Friend	Number of Meals
Dan	|||| |||| //
Sanjay	|||| |||| |||| ///
Andy	|||| ||||

> Tally marks look like slashes. Put the fifth tally across the first four.

What does each tally mark show? _____

What does each group of 5 tally marks show? _____

Write the number of meals each friend cooked.

Dan _____   Sanjay _____   Andy _____

Look at the blank table below. Use it to make your picture graph.

Dan	

Key: ○ = 2 meals

UNIT 6 Measurement and Data

Focused Instruction — Lesson 27

What should the title of the picture graph be? _____

Label the first column.

Fill in the rest of the first column.

Label the second column.

How many meals does each symbol show? _____

What operation should you use to show how to find the number of symbols to put in each row? _____

What number sentence shows how many symbols to draw for Dan?
_____

What number sentence shows how many symbols to draw for Sanjay?
_____

What number sentence shows how many symbols to draw for Andy?
_____

Complete the second column of the picture graph.

Use what you know about picture graphs to answer these questions.

LUNCH

Item	Number Sold
Pizza	$ $ $ $
Burger	$ $ $ $ $ $ $ $
Taco	$ $

Key: $ = 2 items

1 How many pizzas were sold? _____

2 How many burgers were sold? _____

3 How many more pizzas were sold than tacos? _____

Part 3 Guided Practice — Lesson 27

Solve the following problems.

1. This picture graph shows the number of hits by some players on a baseball team.

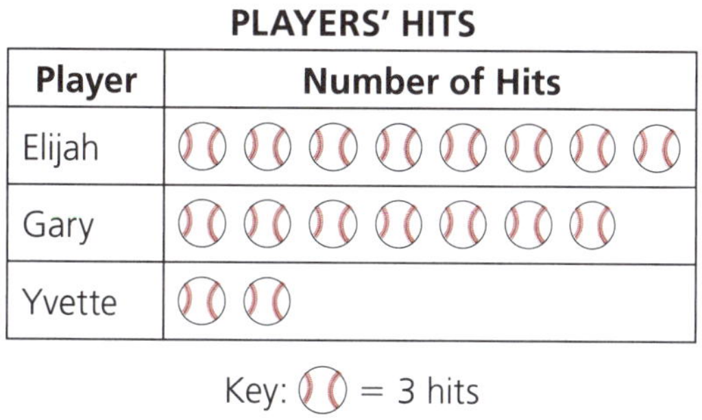

PLAYERS' HITS

Player	Number of Hits
Elijah	🙂🙂🙂🙂🙂🙂🙂🙂🙂
Gary	🙂🙂🙂🙂🙂🙂🙂
Yvette	🙂🙂

Key: 🙂 = 3 hits

How many more hits did Elijah make than Yvette? Show your work.

> Use the key to find the number of hits Elijah and Yvette made.

Answer _____ hits

2. During the summer, Asako went to the beach 12 times. Zach went 15 times. Bella went 9 times. Make a picture graph to show the data.

TRIPS TO BEACH

Person	Number of Trips

Key: _____ = 3 trips

> What does the key tell you about the symbol for this picture graph?

UNIT 6 Measurement and Data

Independent Practice   Lesson 27

Solve the following problems.

Use the picture graph below to answer problems 1 and 2.

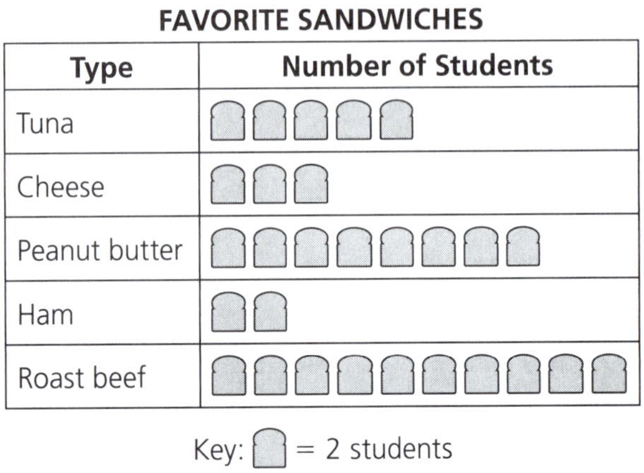

FAVORITE SANDWICHES

Type	Number of Students
Tuna	🍞🍞🍞🍞🍞
Cheese	🍞🍞🍞
Peanut butter	🍞🍞🍞🍞🍞🍞🍞
Ham	🍞🍞
Roast beef	🍞🍞🍞🍞🍞🍞🍞🍞🍞

Key: 🍞 = 2 students

1 Which type of sandwich had the most votes? How many students voted for this sandwich?

   Answer _____

2 There were 14 students who said that chicken sandwiches are their favorite type of sandwich. How many symbols would you use to show this data? Explain.

   _____

   _____

228 UNIT 6 Measurement and Data

Independent Practice

Lesson 27

Use the picture graph below to answer problems 3 and 4.

CORRECT ANSWERS

Student	Number Correct
Grace	★ ★ ★ ★
Nico	★ ★ ★ ★ ★ ★
Vin	★

Key: ★ = 5 correct answers

3 The picture graph shows the number of correct answers students got on a test. How many fewer answers did Vin get correct than Grace?

Answer _____ answers

4 How many correct answers did Nico get on the test?

A 5

B 6

C 30

D 35

UNIT 6 Measurement and Data

Independent Practice

Lesson 27

5 Anya, Sydney, and Bob play the piano. They kept track of the number of hours they each practiced one week. This tally chart shows the information.

PIANO PRACTICE

Friend	Number of Hours
Anya	︎IIII III
Sydney	IIII IIII II
Bob	IIII IIII

Part A Make a picture graph from the tally chart. Be sure to give the picture graph a title and a key.

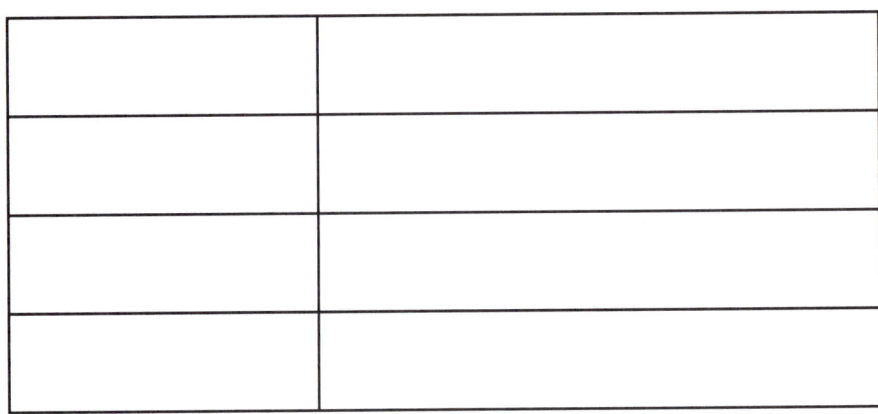

Key: ♪ = _____ hours

Part B The next week, Anya practiced for 18 hours. Use the key you made in Part A. How many symbols do you need to draw to show 18 hours? Explain how you know.

_____

_____

230 UNIT 6 Measurement and Data

Independent Practice — Lesson 27

6 The picture graph below shows the emails Hana received over three hours.

HANA'S EMAILS

Time	Number of Emails
4 to 5 P.M.	✉✉✉✉✉✉
5 to 6 P.M.	✉✉✉✉✉
6 to 7 P.M.	✉✉✉

Key: ✉ = 4 emails

Part A How many emails did Hana receive from 4 to 5 P.M.?

Answer _____ emails

Part B How many **more** emails did Hana receive from 5 to 6 P.M. than from 6 to 7 P.M.?

Answer _____ emails

Part C Hana received 28 emails from 7 to 8 P.M. How many symbols would show this?

Answer _____ symbols

Lesson 28: Bar Graphs

Part 1: Introduction

A **bar graph** displays **data** using bars. The bars can go up and down or sideways. The height or length of each bar tells you how much.

This table shows the numbers of pets students in a class have.

Cats	Dogs	Fish	Other
3	5	5	7

Data is information.

To put this data in a bar graph, think about what the bars will show. There will be one bar for each type of pet.

The **scale** is the numbers on the graph. Choose a scale for your bar graph. The data shows that the least number of a type of pet is 3. The greatest number is 7. You can make your scale from 0 to 10.

Bars that go across are horizontal. Bars that go up and down are vertical.

Draw and label a bar for each type of pet. The top of the bar stops at the correct number on the scale. Be sure to label the sides of the graph. Always give the graph a title.

Sometimes your scale will have a lot of numbers. You can skip count to make it easier to read.

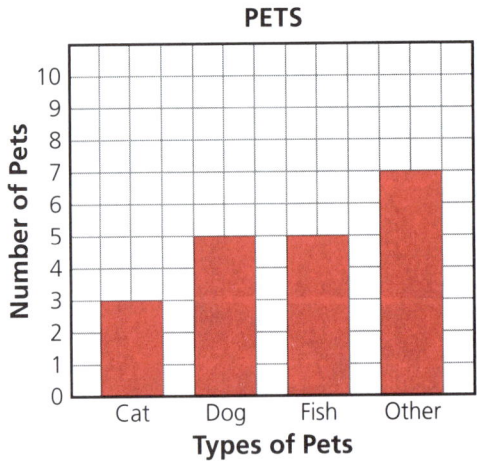

You can compare data by using the heights of the bars. In the bar graph above, the bar for *Cat* is shorter than the bar for *Dog*. That means that there are more dogs as pets than cats. The bar for *Dog* is 2 units taller, so there are 2 more dogs than cats.

The bar for *Dog* is the same height as the bar for *Fish*. That means that there are the same number of dogs as fish.

232 UNIT 6 Measurement and Data

Think About It

How might bar graphs be useful when compared with data tables?

_____

_____

PART 2 Focused Instruction

Make a bar graph to represent colored candies. Work with a partner. Take a handful of colored candies. Choose no more than four colors.

Colors				
Number of Candies				

Write the colors of the candies in the table. Write the number of each color candy you have.

Use the grid below to make a bar graph showing the data in the table.

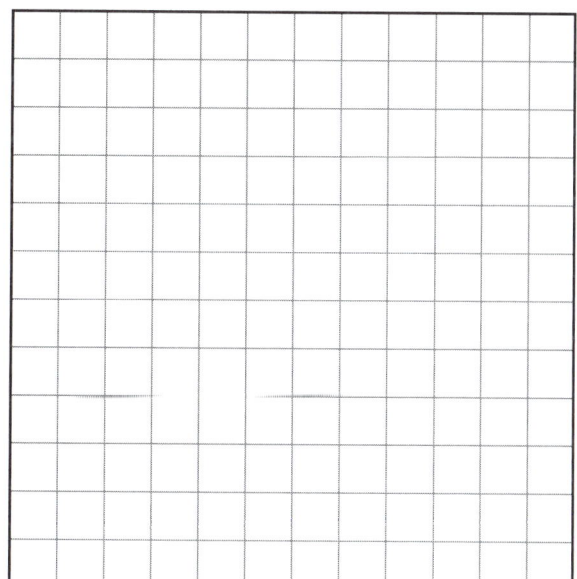

What is the least number of candies? _____ The greatest number? _____

Choose a scale that works for your data. Write the scale on the vertical side.

UNIT 6 Measurement and Data **233**

Focused Instruction — Lesson 28

Draw a bar for each color. Label the bars. Be sure to label the horizontal side. Give the bar graph a title.

It is important to read a bar graph carefully. If you do not understand the graph, you will not be able to understand the data in it.

This bar graph shows the number of glasses of different types of juice some people drank one morning.

Look at the scale. What numbers are missing?

_____

What does it mean if a bar ends between two numbers on the scale?

_____

_____

What number is between 8 and 10?

How many people had apple juice? _____

Orange juice? _____

What was the total number of people who had apple or orange juice? _____

How many people had pineapple juice? _____ Grape juice? _____

What was the total number of people who had pineapple or grape juice? _____

What operation should you use to find a difference? _____

How many more people drank apple and orange juice than drank pineapple and grape juice? _____

Use what you know about bar graphs to answer these questions.

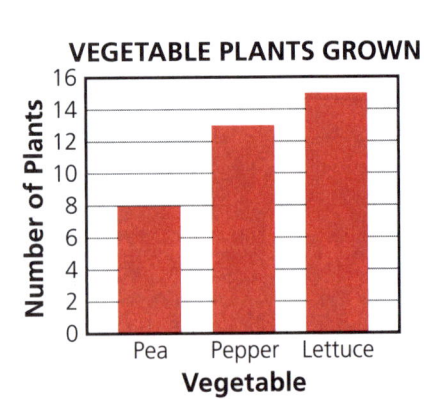

1. How many pepper plants were grown? _____

2. How many more lettuce plants than pea plants were grown? _____

3. How many plants were grown in all? _____

UNIT 6 Measurement and Data

Guided Practice

Lesson 28

Solve the following problems.

1. The table below shows the favorite ice cream flavors of students in a third-grade class. Use the table below to make a bar graph.

FAVORITE ICE CREAM FLAVOR

Ice Cream Flavor	Vanilla	Chocolate	Strawberry
Number of Students	6	15	3

First, decide what scale to use. Then label the scale.

2. The bar graph shows the number of baseball caps some students own.

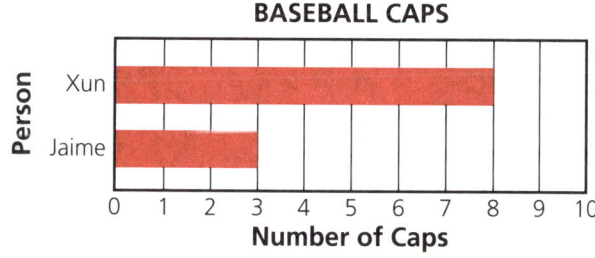

How many more caps does Xun have than Jaime?

Answer _____ caps

What operation do you use to find how many more?

Independent Practice

Lesson 28

Solve the following problems.

1. This bar graph shows how many inches of snow fell each day one week.

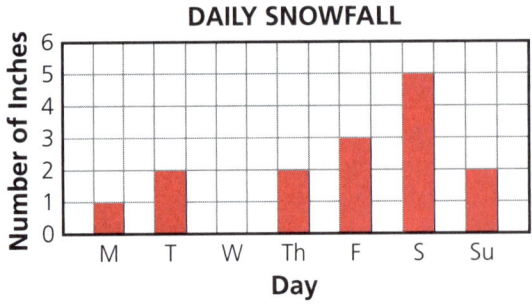

Part A Which of the following statements are true? Select the **three** correct answers.

A. Three more inches of snow fell on Thursday than on Saturday.

B. The same amount of snow fell on Tuesday and Thursday.

C. Eight inches of snow fell on Friday and Saturday.

D. Four more inches of snow fell on Saturday than on Wednesday.

E. Four inches of snow fell on Monday and Tuesday.

F. Five inches of snow fell on Thursday and Friday.

Part B Fill in the blanks to make the following statement correct.

On Monday and Tuesday, _____ inches of snow fell. On Thursday through Sunday, _____ inches of snow fell. So a total of _____ inches of snow fell.

Independent Practice — Lesson 28

2 Which bar graph shows the data in the tally chart?

FLOWERS PLANTED

Girl	Number of Flowers
Anna	||||	
Micaela	///
Sierra	||||

A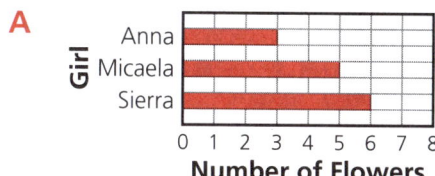

B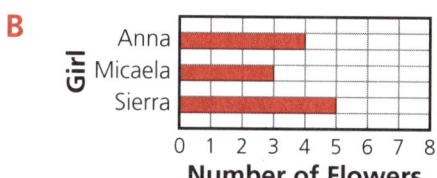

C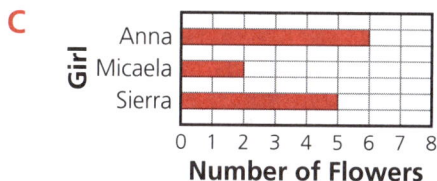

D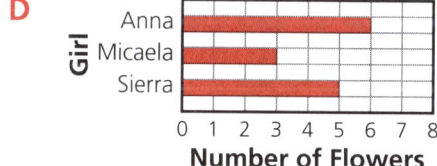

3 The bar graph below shows the number of students who bought hot lunch at Eastbrook Elementary School each day one week.

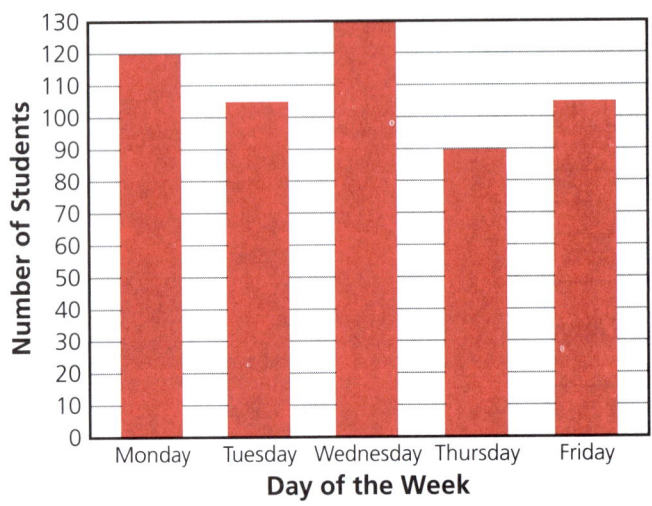

Part A How many more students bought hot lunch on Monday than on Thursday?

Answer _____ students

Part B There are 358 students in the elementary school. How many students did **not** buy hot lunch on Friday?

Answer _____ students

Independent Practice — Lesson 28

4 The students at Strawberry Hill Elementary School had a shoe drive. They collected shoes to help children who need shoes. The picture graph below displays the number of pairs of shoes collected and their sizes.

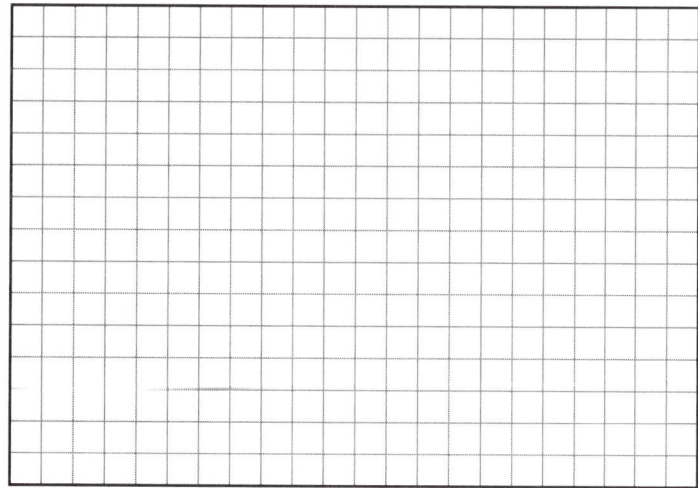

Part A Make a bar graph that shows the data in the table.

Part B How many pairs of shoes were collected in total?

Answer _____ pairs of shoes

Independent Practice — Lesson 28

5 The table below shows the number of goals three teams scored at a soccer tournament.

SOCCER TOURNAMENT

Team	Number of Goals
Tigers	4
Streaks	9
Rays	7

Make a bar graph to show this data. Remember to label your graph. Give your graph a title.

LESSON 29: Measurement Data on Line Plots

CCLS: 3.MD.4

Part 1 Introduction

Many lengths can be measured with a inch ruler. The measurements you make are **data,** or information. One way to show measurement data is in a **line plot.**

A line plot starts with a number line. Use an X or dot above a number on the number line to show a measurement. Use one X or dot for each measurement.

The Washington family went fishing last weekend. They measured the length of each fish they caught.

Length of Fish Caught (inches)
12, 11, 10, 4, 5, 12, 11, 5, 12, 8, 12, 4, 10

First, draw a number line that includes all of the measurements.

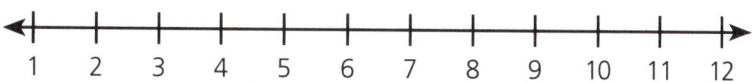

> When you make the number line, include all numbers between the least value and greatest value.

Then draw an X above the length for each fish caught. Start with the lowest number. They caught 2 fish that were 4 inches long. Draw 2 Xs above the 4. They also caught 2 fish that were 5 inches long. Draw 2 Xs above the 5. Draw an X for every measurement.

FISHING TRIP

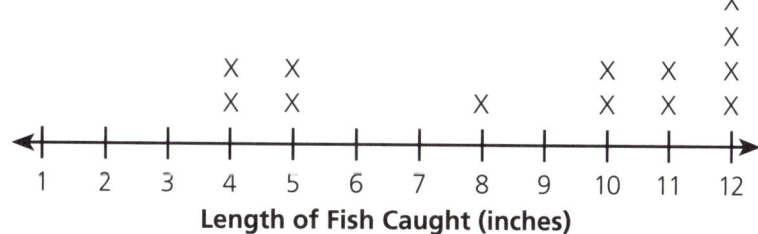

Length of Fish Caught (inches)

> Cross out the measurements as you add them to the plot. This way you will not miss any.

Think About It

How is a line plot useful for looking at data? Explain.

_____

_____

UNIT 6 Measurement and Data **241**

Focused Instruction — Lesson 29

Sometimes measurements are given using fractions. Be sure that the number line includes the fractions when you make a line plot. Always look at the data carefully.

Mr. Ruiz's class grew sunflowers. They measured how tall the sunflowers grew.

SUNFLOWER HEIGHTS (feet)

| $6\frac{1}{4}$ | $5\frac{3}{4}$ | $6\frac{1}{2}$ | 6 | $5\frac{1}{4}$ | 5 | $7\frac{1}{4}$ | 6 | $6\frac{1}{4}$ | 6 | 7 | $6\frac{1}{2}$ | 6 | $7\frac{1}{4}$ | $5\frac{3}{4}$ |

What will be the lowest number on your number line? _____

What will be the highest number on your number line? _____

What fractions do you need to put on your number line? _____

Label the numbers on the number line.

> The numbers on a number line should be in equal steps. That means the differences between the numbers are the same.

Find the first measurement from the box on the number line. Draw an X above it.

Continue until you have drawn an X for every measurement. Give the line plot a title.

Look at the line plot. Use it to understand the data.

What is the height of the tallest sunflower? How do you know?

_____

What is the height of the shortest sunflower? How do you know?

_____

Which height occurred most often?

_____

> Look for the measurement with the greatest number of Xs over it.

Focused Instruction

Lesson 29

Work with a partner to measure objects. Collect 10 pens, pencils, markers, or crayons. Measure the objects. Then show your results on a line plot.

Measure the length of each object to the nearest half inch. Write the measurements in the space below.

> Look at a ruler carefully. The mark directly between two inch-marks is the half-inch mark.
>
> $\frac{1}{2}$ inch

Use the number line below to make a line plot.

What is the smallest number you will use on your number line? _____

What is the greatest number? _____

What fractions will you need to put on your number line?
_____

> Make sure you include all the measurements on your line plot.

Complete the line plot using your data.

Use what you know about line plots to answer these questions.

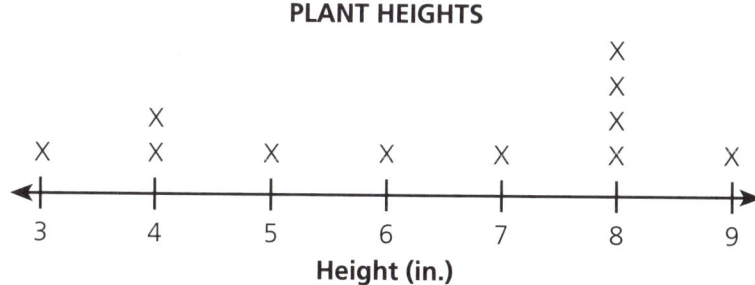

1. What was the most common height? _____

2. What is the difference between the tallest and the shortest plant? _____

UNIT 6 Measurement and Data

Guided Practice — Lesson 29

Solve the following problems.

1 Suki measured the ribbons below to the nearest $\frac{1}{2}$ inch.

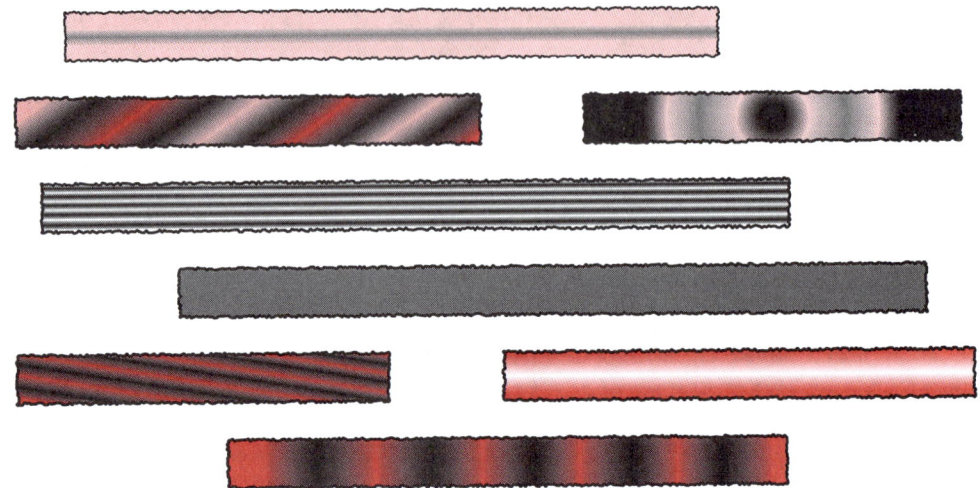

Use the number line below to make a line plot showing the lengths of these ribbons. Remember to give the line plot a title. Label the number line.

> Each measurement is shown by an X.

2 Rafael visited a farm. He measured the lengths, in inches, of several watermelons.

$$12,\ 18,\ 16\tfrac{1}{2},\ 10\tfrac{3}{4},\ 14\tfrac{1}{4},\ 16\tfrac{1}{2},\ 15,\ 14\tfrac{1}{4},\ 16\tfrac{1}{2}$$

He makes a line plot to show his data. Which length will have exactly 2 Xs above it?

Answer _____ inches

> Measurements that are the same each get an X over that number on the number line.

Independent Practice

Lesson 29

Solve the following problems.

1. Kara measured the lengths of some leaves that fell from a tree. The lengths are shown below.

   LENGTH OF LEAF (inches)

$2\frac{1}{2}$	$3\frac{3}{4}$	$3\frac{1}{2}$	$2\frac{3}{4}$	3	$3\frac{1}{4}$	4	$2\frac{1}{4}$
$3\frac{1}{4}$	2	$3\frac{1}{4}$	3	4	$2\frac{1}{2}$	3	

   Part A Make a line plot to show the data.

   Part B What is the difference between the longest leaf's length and the shortest leaf's length?

   Answer _____ inches

UNIT 6 Measurement and Data

Independent Practice — Lesson 29

2 Blake cuts out strips of paper for a project. Some of the strips are shown below.

A
B
C
D

Part A What is the length of each strip of paper to the nearest $\frac{1}{4}$ inch?

Paper A _____ inches

Paper B _____ inches

Paper C _____ inches

Paper D _____ inches

Part B Blake needed several strips of paper for his project. He made this table to show the number of strips of paper the same length as those shown above.

Strip of Paper	Number of Strips
A	3
B	5
C	2
D	3

Use the data from Part A and the table to make a line plot.

UNIT 6 Measurement and Data

Independent Practice — Lesson 29

3 Terry wrote down the lengths, in inches, of ten worms.

$$3\frac{1}{2}, 5, 4, 4\frac{1}{2}, 4, 3, 6\frac{1}{2}, 3, 4, 3\frac{1}{2}$$

Which line plot shows this data?

A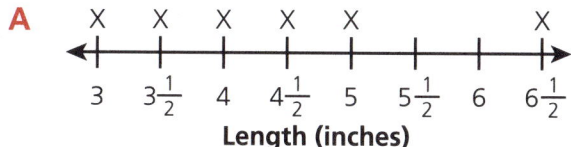

B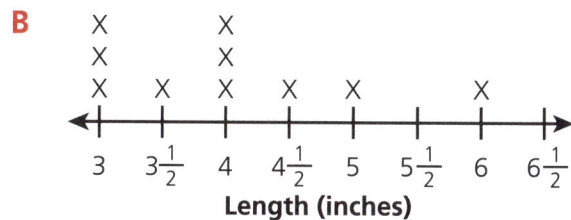

C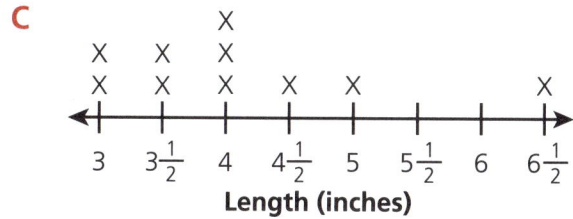

D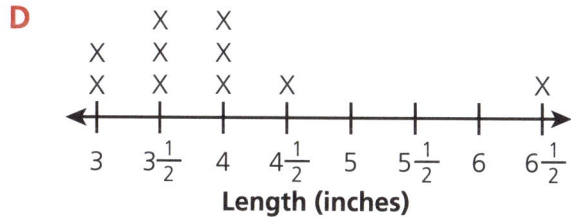

Independent Practice — Lesson 29

4 The data set below shows the lengths, in inches, of some cats' tails.

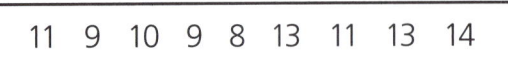

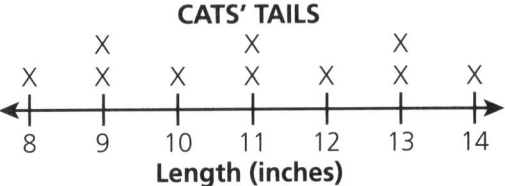

Jen made the line plot at the right for the data set. Is her line plot correct? Explain.

_____

_____

5 Hatsu and some of her friends are making beaded necklaces. They measure the length of each necklace. The lengths, in inches, are shown below.

$12\frac{1}{2}$	15	$18\frac{1}{2}$	15	14	$17\frac{1}{2}$	18	$15\frac{1}{2}$
$18\frac{1}{2}$	14	14	15	$14\frac{1}{2}$	18	16	

Use the number line below to make a line plot with this data. Give the line plot a title. Label the line plot.

Lesson 30: Understanding Area

CCLS: 3.MD.5.a, b; 6

Part 1 Introduction

A **plane figure** is a flat surface. The size of the space inside the plane figure is its **area.** One way to measure area is to count the number of square units that cover a figure. A **square unit** is a square with a side of 1 unit. As long as the square units do not have gaps between them or overlap, the number of square units is the area of the figure.

> Area is always measured in square units.

Look at the figure in red on the grid below.

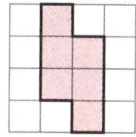 = 1 square unit

The red figure is made up of 6 square units. Its area is 6 square units.

A unit can be any measurement used for length. A square unit may stand for a square inch, square foot, or another square unit.

What is the area of the figure in red?

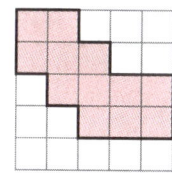 = 1 square centimeter

Look at the key on the right. It shows that 1 square unit is equal to 1 square centimeter. The red figure is made up of 12 square units. So, its area is 12 square centimeters.

Think About It

Why might it be important to measure the area of something? What might area help you understand?

_____

_____

UNIT 6 Measurement and Data 249

Focused Instruction

Lesson 30

When figures are drawn on grids, you can see the square units inside. Always look at the key to see what each square unit shows.

Two students are each asked to draw a figure with an area of 8 square inches. Which student, if either, is correct?

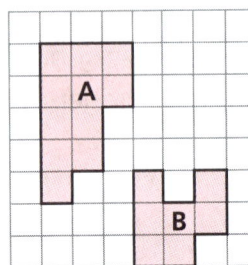

☐ = 1 square inch

What is the area of each square unit? _____

How can you find the area of each figure?

_____

How many squares cover the figure student A made? _____

What is the area of student A's figure? _____

How many squares cover the figure student B made? _____

What is the area of student B's figure? _____

Did either student make a figure with an area of 8 square inches? _____

How can student A correct the figure to make it have the correct area?

_____

How can student B correct the figure to make it have the correct area?

_____

> Count the squares inside the figures.

> Is the area greater than 8 square inches or less?

UNIT 6 Measurement and Data

Focused Instruction — Lesson 30

Use a grid to draw a figure with a certain area.

Draw a figure with an area of 15 square units.

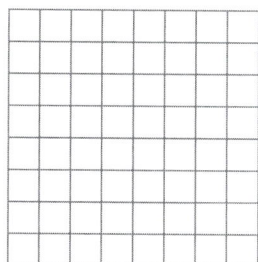 ☐ = 1 square unit

What is the area of each square on the grid? _____

How can you show a figure with an area of 15 square units?

_____

Can the squares in the figure overlap? _____

Can you leave spaces between the squares in the figure? _____

Draw a figure with an area of 15 square units.

Use what you know about area to answer these questions about the figure below.

☐ = 1 square foot

1 What is the area of each square unit? _____

2 What is the area of the rectangle? _____

UNIT 6 Measurement and Data

Guided Practice

Solve the following problems.

1. On the grid below, draw a figure that has an area of 40 square units.

   Remember that unit squares cannot have gaps or overlap.

2. What is the area of the figure?

   = 1 square unit

   Count the number of unit squares that make up the figure.

   Answer _____ square units

3. What is the area of the figure?

   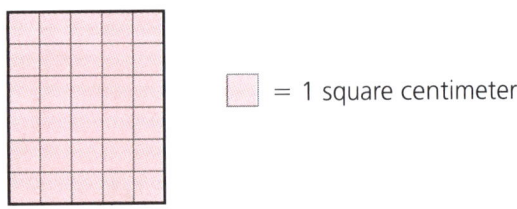
   = 1 square centimeter

   How many rows of squares are there? How many squares are in each row?

   Answer _____ square centimeters

UNIT 6 Measurement and Data

Independent Practice

Lesson 30

Solve the following problems.

1. Pablo is measuring the area of a plane figure. He is using a unit square with a side length of 1 yard. What is the area of 1 square unit?

   Answer _____

2. What is the area of the shaded figure?

   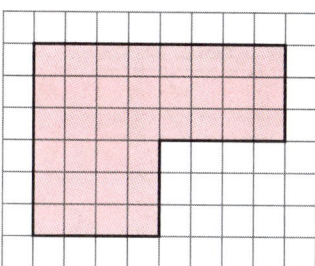

   A 12 square units

   B 24 square units

   C 36 square units

   D 48 square units

3. What is the area of the figure?

   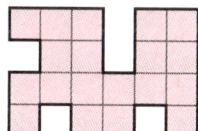

   Answer _____ square units

UNIT 6 Measurement and Data

Independent Practice — Lesson 30

4 Each square in each shape measures 1 square centimeter. Put each shape in the correct part of the table by matching its area.

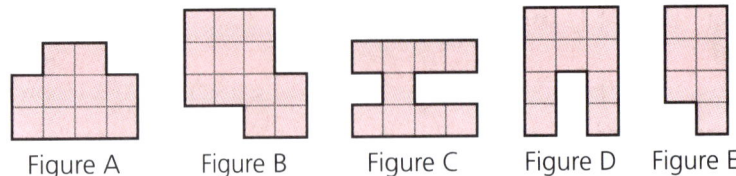

Figure A   Figure B   Figure C   Figure D   Figure E

Area Is Smaller Than 10 Square Centimeters	Area Is 10 Square Centimeters	Area Is Larger Than 10 Square Centimeters

5 Each square unit on the grid has a side of 1 meter.

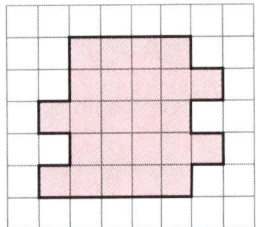

What is the area of the shaded figure?

A 20 square meters

B 22 square meters

C 24 square meters

D 26 square meters

6 Look at the figure on the grid at the right. What is the area of this figure?

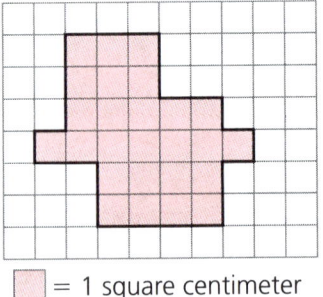

= 1 square centimeter

Answer _____ square centimeters

UNIT 6 Measurement and Data

Lesson 30

7 A photographer made a display of photographs. She covered a wall with 50 square photographs. The entire wall was covered without gaps or overlaps. Each photograph is 1 foot long on each side. What is the area of the wall? Explain how you know.

_____

_____

_____

8 Tiana measured the area of a piece of paper shaped like a plane figure as shown. She placed squares units on the paper. Tiana found the area to be 6 square units.

☐ = 1 square unit

What error did Tiana make?

_____

_____

UNIT 6 Measurement and Data

LESSON 31: Multiplying to Find Area

Part 1 Introduction

A **plane figure** is a flat shape. **Area** is a measure of the space inside the figure. In Lesson 30, you learned to measure area by covering the plane figure with unit squares. For rectangles and squares, you can use another method as well. You can multiply the length by the width.

What is the area of the rectangle?

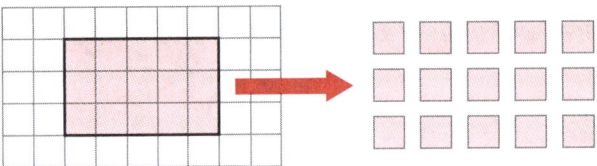

Count the unit squares that cover the rectangle. There are 15 in all. So the area is 15 square units.

Now look again at the unit squares. There are 3 rows of 5 unit squares. Multiply:

$$3 \times 5 = 15$$

The area is 15 square units. Both methods give the same result.

> Think of the unit squares in a rectangle as an array.

Most of the time, you will not see the square units in a figure. You will only know the measurements.

What is the area of the rectangle?

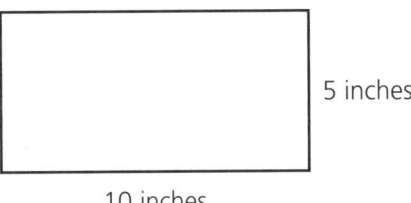

5 inches
10 inches

The rectangle is 5 inches wide and 10 inches long. This means if the rectangle were covered by unit squares, there would be 5 rows of 10 unit squares. Multiply:

$$5 \times 10 = 50 \text{ square inches}$$

UNIT 6 Measurement and Data

Think About It

What is something someone might need to know the area of in real life? Why?

_____

_____

_____

 Focused Instruction

You can use square tiles to help you understand area. Work with a partner.

Cut a piece of paper so that you have a rectangle that measures 6 inches long and 5 inches wide.

What is the length of the rectangle? _____

Label the length on your rectangle.

What is the width of the rectangle? _____

Label the width on your rectangle.

Use your square tiles. Cover your rectangle with unit squares.

How many unit squares can you use to cover the rectangle? _____

What is the area of the rectangle? _____

How else can you find the area without using unit squares?

_____

Use the other method to find the area. Show your work.

Did you find the same area using both methods? _____

UNIT 6 Measurement and Data

Focused Instruction — Lesson 31

Sometimes it helps to draw a picture. Use a picture to help you solve this problem.

Samson is painting the roof of a birdhouse. The roof is 8 inches long and 7 inches wide. He has enough craft paint left to cover 50 square inches.

On a separate piece of paper, draw the roof of the birdhouse. Label the length and width.

Draw grid lines on the roof to divide it into equal squares. Make the side of each square 1 inch.

How many inches long is the roof? _____

How many inches wide is the roof? _____

How many squares did you draw on the roof? _____

What operation can you use to find the area? _____

Find the area using this operation.

_____

Did you get the same area as when you counted squares? _____

Use what you know about area to answer these questions.

1. Keaton's poster is 15 inches long and 10 inches wide. How many square-inch tiles could he cover it with? _____

2. Mariah drew a rectangle on the playground with chalk. It is 5 feet long and 4 feet wide. What is the area of the rectangle? _____

258 UNIT 6 Measurement and Data

Guided Practice — Lesson 31

Solve the following problems.

1. What is the area of the rectangle below?

   7 ft
   4 ft

   > The area of a rectangle can be found using length times width.

   Answer _____ square feet

2. Alex has a rectangular office that is 7 feet wide and 9 feet long. He wants to cover the floor with carpet. What is the area of Alex's office floor? Show your work.

   > Remember that you can always draw a picture to help you solve a problem.

   Answer _____ square feet

3. Which two rectangles have the same area?

   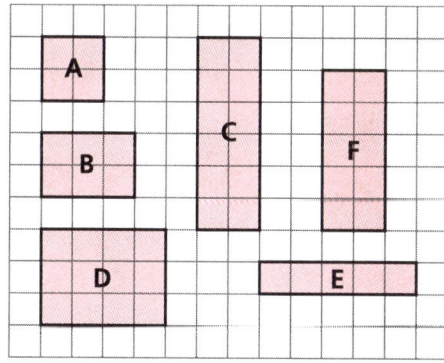

   > Figures can have the same area but not look the same.

   Answer _____

UNIT 6 Measurement and Data

Independent Practice

Lesson 31

Solve the following problems.

1 Which expression can you use to find the area of the rectangle shown?

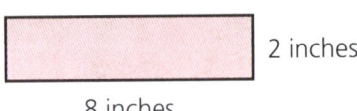
2 inches
8 inches

A 8 × 8

B 8 + 2

C 8 × 2

D 8 + 8 + 2 + 2

2 Draw a unit grid to find the area of the rectangle at the right. How does the area you found compare with the area found by multiplying? Explain.

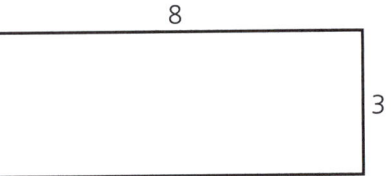

_____
_____
_____
_____

3 Celia is covering her kitchen floor with tiles that are each 1 square foot. The floor is in the shape of a rectangle that is 6 feet wide and 9 feet long. How many tiles does she need to cover the entire kitchen floor?

Answer _____ tiles

4 Which equation shows the area of the shaded rectangle?

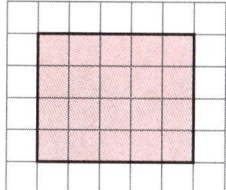

A 4 × 5 = 20

B 4 + 5 = 9

C 4 + 5 + 4 + 5 = 18

D 4 × 4 = 16

5 Sally built a puzzle using 42 square units. What are possible dimensions of the puzzle?

Answer _____

6 Archie wants to cover the top of his model table with colored paper. The top of the table is shown.

How many square centimeters of paper does Archie need if each square equals 1 square centimeter?

Answer _____ square centimeters

Independent Practice — Lesson 31

7 The National September 11 Memorial includes 2 reflecting pools. Each pool is a square that measures about 60 yards on each side. What is the area covered by both reflecting pools? Show your work.

Answer _____ square feet

8 Alyssa wants to wallpaper one wall of her living room. The wall is 9 feet high and 18 feet long.

Part A How many square feet of wallpaper will Alyssa need to cover the wall? Show your work.

Answer _____

Part B The wallpaper Alyssa has chosen comes in rolls that are 3 feet wide and 24 feet long. How many rolls of wallpaper will Alyssa need to cover the wall? Explain.

_____
_____
_____
_____

LESSON 32: Adding to Find Area

CCLS: 3.MD.7.c, d

Part 1 Introduction

You have been learning different ways to find the **area** of a rectangle. You can tile the rectangle with unit squares and count them. You can multiply the length by the width. Sometimes the **distributive property** can help you find the area.

Find the area of the large rectangle.

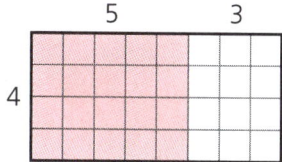

The length of the rectangle in units is 5 + 3. The width of the rectangle is 4 units. In order to find the area, you multiply the length by the width.

$$4 \times (5 + 3) =$$
$$(4 \times 5) + (4 \times 3) = 20 + 12$$
$$= 32 \text{ square units}$$

The area is the sum of the areas of the two rectangles (shaded and not shaded).

> The distributive property says that multiplying a number by a sum is the same as multiplying each number in the sum.
> $a \times (b + c) = (a \times b) + (a \times c)$
> $4 \times (3 + 1) = (4 \times 3) + (4 \times 1)$
> $4 \times 4 = 12 + 4$
> $16 = 16$

Some figures are not rectangles, but they can be split into rectangles. You can find the area of each rectangle. Then add them together.

The lengths of the sides of the figure are shown in centimeters (cm). Find the area of the figure.

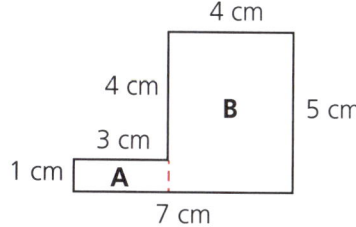

UNIT 6 Measurement and Data **263**

Make two rectangles, A and B, by drawing a line across the figure.

Find the area of rectangle A: 3 cm × 1 cm = 3 sq cm
Find the area of rectangle B: 4 cm × 5 cm = 20 sq cm

Add to find the total: 3 sq cm + 20 sq cm = 23 sq cm

The area of the figure is 23 square centimeters.

> You can write sq to mean *square*.

Think About It

Why do you think it is important to know how to find area of things that are made up of rectangles?

_____
_____
_____
_____

2 Focused Instruction

Multiply the length and the width to find the area of a rectangle. Sometimes you may need to find the length of a missing side. Look at the other side lengths. Think about what you know about rectangles.

This figure is made up of two rectangles.

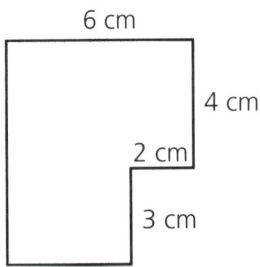

Draw a horizontal line to divide the figure into two rectangles. Label the top rectangle A and the bottom B.

What is the length of rectangle A? _____ What is the width? _____

> Which line would you extend to divide the figure horizontally?

264 UNIT 6 Measurement and Data

Focused Instruction

Lesson 32

What is the area of rectangle A? _____

The picture does not show the length of rectangle B. Look for the length of rectangle A. Is rectangle B longer or shorter than rectangle A? _____

> Area = length × width

Look carefully at the picture. Can you find a given length that you can use with the length of rectangle A to find the length of rectangle B? Explain.

_____
_____

What is the length of rectangle B? _____ What is the width of rectangle B? _____

What is the area of rectangle B? _____

How do you find the area of the entire figure?

_____

What is the area of the entire figure? _____

Use what you know about area to answer these questions.

1. A figure is made up of two rectangles. The area of one rectangle is 12 square inches. The area of the other rectangle is 8 square inches. What is the total area of the figure?

   _____

2. A rectangle is 2 meters wide and 5 + 3 meters long.

   What is the area of the rectangle? _____

Guided Practice — Lesson 32

Solve the following problems.

1. Find the area of the figure.

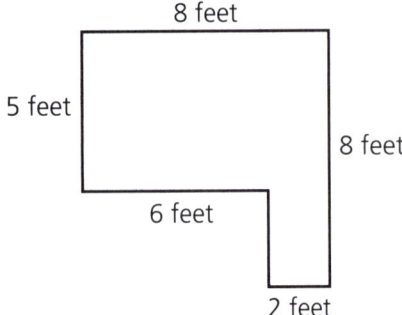

> Divide the figure into two rectangles.

Answer _____ square feet

2. Fill in the equation to show the area of the rectangle below.

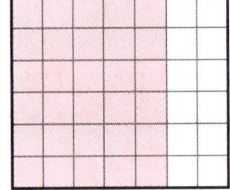

> Use the distributive property to solve.

Answer _____ × (_____ + 2) = _____ square units

Independent Practice

Lesson 32

Solve the following problems.

1 Find the area of the figure below.

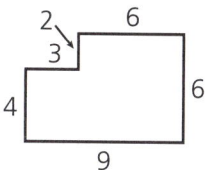

- **A** 24 square units
- **B** 36 square units
- **C** 48 square units
- **D** 54 square units

2 Which area model shows that 5 × (2 + 1) = (5 × 2) + (5 × 1) is true?

A

B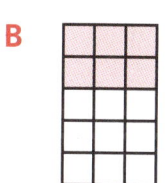

C

D

Independent Practice

Lesson 32

3 The area of the white rectangle is 27 square inches. The area of the red rectangle is 10 square inches.

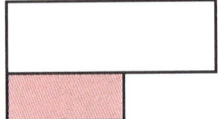

What is the area of the whole figure?

A 17 square inches

B 37 square inches

C 45 square inches

D 54 square inches

4 A floor plan for Wendy's apartment is shown at the right. Including the patio, the apartment measures 664 square feet. What is the area of the patio? Show your work.

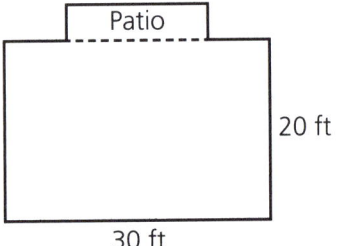

Answer _____ square feet

Independent Practice — Lesson 32

5 Ronit is covering a table with tiles to make the design shown.

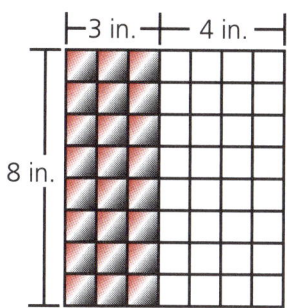

Which expressions could be used to find the area, in square inches? Select the **two** correct answers.

A (8 × 3) + (8 × 4)

B (8 + 3) × (8 + 4)

C 3 × 4 × 8

D 8 × (3 + 4)

E 3 + 4 + 8

F 8 + (3 × 4)

6 Yelena cuts a piece of plastic to seal the window around her air conditioner. The picture at the right shows the piece of plastic. What is the area of the piece of plastic?

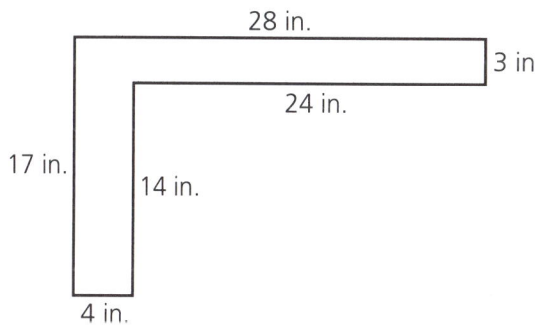

Answer _____ square inches

Independent Practice — Lesson 32

7 Isabel and Amanda planted corn and peas. Their garden plot is shown below.

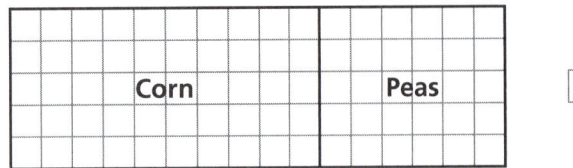

= 1 square yard

The girls want to find the area of their garden plot.

Amanda plans to find the areas of both rectangles and add them together to find the total area. Isabel plans to measure the length and the width of the entire garden to find the area.

Whose way is correct? Explain your reasoning and find the area of the entire garden.

LESSON 33: Perimeter and Area

CCLS: 3.MD.8

Part 1 Introduction

Area is a measure of the amount of space inside a plane figure. **Perimeter** is the distance around the outside of the figure. Perimeter is measured in units of length, such as inches, feet, and centimeters.

What is the perimeter of the figure shown?

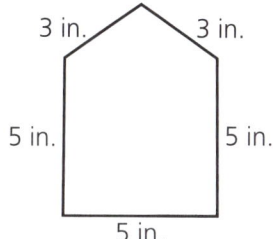

> Add the lengths of the sides to find perimeter.

Perimeter = 3 in. + 3 in. + 5 in. + 5 in. + 5 in.
= 21 in.

The perimeter of the pentagon is 21 inches.

Figures can have the same perimeter but different areas. They can also have the same areas but different perimeters.

Compare the perimeters and areas of these rectangles.

4 in.	6 in.
3 in. [A] 3 in.	2 in. [B] 2 in.
4 in.	6 in.

Rectangle A
Perimeter = 3 + 3 + 4 + 4 = 14 in.
Area = 3 × 4 = 12 sq in.

Rectangle B
Perimeter = 2 + 2 + 6 + 6 = 16 in.
Area = 2 × 6 = 12 sq in.

The rectangles have different perimeters but the same area.

UNIT 6 Measurement and Data **271**

Think About It

In real life, when might you use perimeter instead of area? Explain.

_____

_____

_____

_____

PART 2 Focused Instruction

Find the perimeter of a figure to help you solve problems.

Ramon is fencing in his backyard. He drew a diagram of his backyard and measured the sides. The fencing he is using costs $10 per foot.

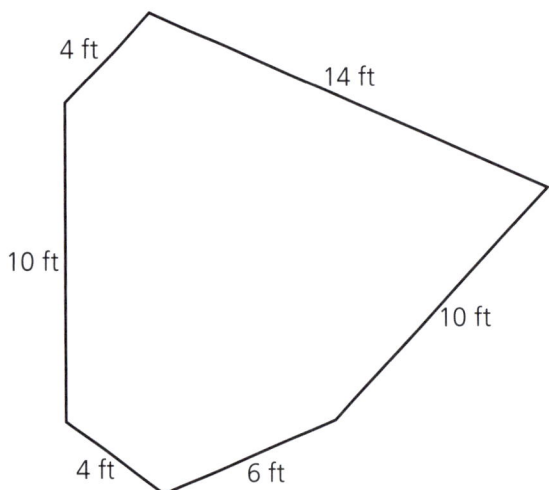

Does Ramon need to find perimeter or area? _____

How can Ramon find the total amount of fence he needs?

_____

How much fencing will he need? _____

How can Ramon find the total cost?

_____

How much will it cost Ramon to buy the fence? _____

272 UNIT 6 Measurement and Data

Lesson 33

Sometimes you know the perimeter of a figure. You must find the length of a missing side. Use information about perimeter to solve the problem.

Look at the figure below.

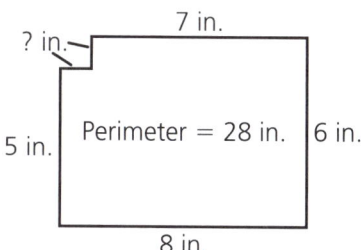

> Count the sides of the figure. Make sure you add this number of lengths together.

How do you find the perimeter of a figure?
_____

What is the perimeter of this figure? _____

Add to find the length of the sides you know. _____

How could you find the missing measurements?
_____

Fill in this equation to help you find the total length of the missing sides.

_____ inches − _____ inches = _____ inches

What is the total length of the missing sides? _____

Use what you know about perimeter to answer the questions.

1. A rectangle has a width of 2 centimeters. Its perimeter is 12 centimeters. What is its length? _____

2. A square has a side length of 4 inches. What is the perimeter of the square? _____

UNIT 6 Measurement and Data **273**

Guided Practice

Lesson 33

Solve the following problems.

1. Mr. Bernillo drew this plan for a new kennel for his dog.

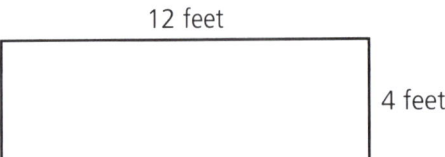

What is the perimeter of the kennel?

> Perimeter is the sum of the lengths of the sides.

Answer _____ feet

2. The perimeter of this figure is 24 feet.

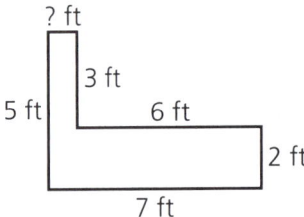

Part A Find the length of the missing side of this figure.

> First, find the sum of the known sides.

Answer _____ ft

Part B In the space below, draw a rectangle with the same perimeter as the figure above. Label the sides.

UNIT 6 Measurement and Data

Independent Practice   Lesson 33

Solve the following problems.

1. A rectangle is 12 inches long and 5 inches wide. What is its perimeter?

   A 17 inches

   B 22 inches

   C 34 inches

   D 60 inches

2. What is the perimeter of the figure on the grid below?

   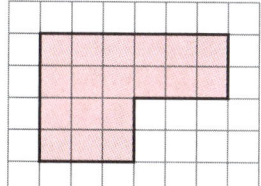

   A 18 units

   B 20 units

   C 24 units

   D 26 units

3. A volleyball court forms a rectangle that is divided in half by the net. Look at the drawing. Find the perimeter of the volleyball court.

   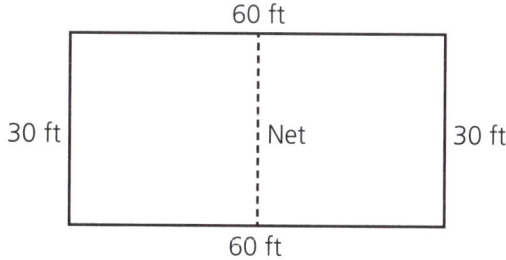

   Answer _____ feet

UNIT 6 Measurement and Data

PART 4 Independent Practice — Lesson 33

4 Which figure has the same perimeter as the figure below?

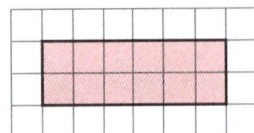

A

B

C

D

Independent Practice — Lesson 33

5 Marty plans to plant a garden. He wants the garden to have an area of 30 square yards. Marty will enclose the garden with a fence. He has 25 yards of fencing.

Part A Marty marks a rectangle on the ground that is 3 yards wide and 10 yards long. Does he have enough fencing to enclose that rectangle? Explain.

Part B Draw and label a rectangle with an area of 30 square yards that Marty can enclose with 25 yards of fencing or less. Explain why your answer is correct.

Part 4 Independent Practice — Lesson 33

6 Ashley is decorating a box. She has 24 inches of ribbon that she wants to put around the box. What are the side lengths of a rectangular box she can buy to use all the ribbon?

Answer _____ inches

7 Maya said, "I have two different rectangles with equal perimeters, so they must have equal areas." Is Maya correct? In the space below, use pictures, numbers, and words to explain why or why not.

_____
_____
_____
_____

UNIT 6 REVIEW
Measurement and Data

CCLS: 3.MD.1–8

1. Denzel ran for 22 minutes. Emmitt ran 7 minutes longer than Denzel. Irvin ran 12 minutes less than Emmitt. How many minutes did Irvin run?

   A 3
   B 17
   C 27
   D 41

2. Claire was at the frozen yogurt shop in town. She filled her cup with yogurt and her favorite toppings.

   How much did Claire's cup of yogurt and toppings weigh?

   A 250 grams
   B 275 grams
   C 325 grams
   D 350 grams

3 Dashi made this drawing in art class.

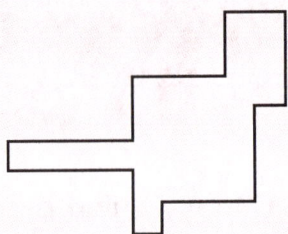

Which type of unit could Dashi use to find the area of her drawing?

A ○

B —

C △

D □

4 The perimeter of a triangle is 44 inches. One side is 14 inches long. Another side is 12 inches long. How long is the third side? Show your work.

Answer _____ inches

5 A tennis court forms a rectangle. A court is 26 yards long and 9 yards wide. What is its area? Show your work.

Answer _____ square yards

6 Heather built a slate patio at her house. The patio is shown at the right. What is the area of the patio?

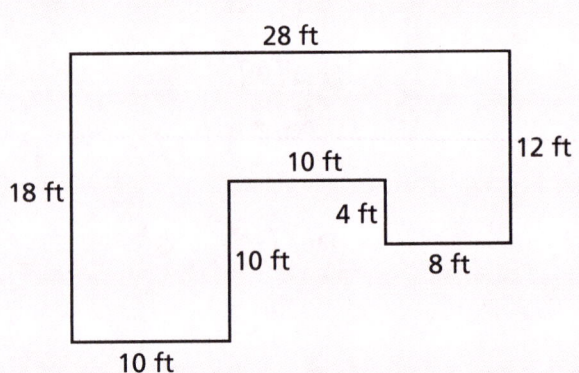

Answer _____ square feet

7 Jordan collected some feathers. Some of the feathers are shown below.

A _____ inches

B _____ inches

C _____ inches

D _____ inches

E _____ inches

Part A Measure the length in inches of each feather. Write the length next to each feather.

Part B Jordan found two more feathers that were the same length as feather B. He found one more that was the same length as feather D, and one that was the same length as feather A. Make a line plot showing the lengths of all of Jordan's feathers. Remember to give your line plot a title.

8 Mrs. Alvarez is having a party. She will put two tables together. The top of table A is a rectangle that is 5 feet long and 3 feet wide.

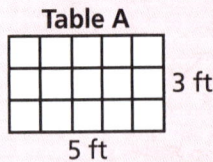

Table A
3 ft
5 ft

Part A What is the area of table A?

Answer _____ square feet

Part B Table B is longer than table A. Table B has the same width as table A, but is 10 feet long. Find the total area of the tabletop when both tables are pushed together. Show your work.

Answer _____ square feet

Part C Mrs. Alvarez has a roll of paper that covers 54 square feet. She pushes a third table, table C, next to table B. Her roll of paper exactly covers all three tables. What is the area of the top of table C? Show your work.

Answer _____ square feet

9 Jasmine plans to tile her bathroom. Jasmine's bathroom is shown below. The shaded area shows the floor outside the shower. The non-shaded area shows the floor inside the shower. The tiles each measure 1 foot on each side.

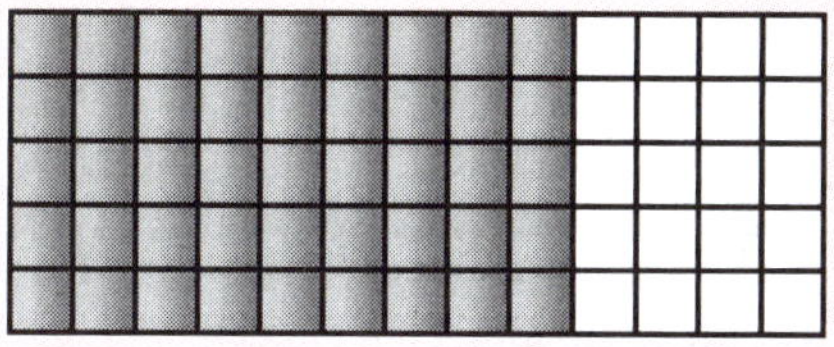

Part A Write an expression to find the area of the entire bathroom floor, including the part in the shower.

Answer _____

Part B Find the area of the entire bathroom floor.

Answer _____ square feet

Part C Jasmine has 100 square feet of tiles. She is only putting tiles on the shaded area. After she puts tiles on the floor of the bathroom, not including the shower floor, how many square feet of tiles will Jasmine have left?

Answer _____ square feet

Part D Next, Jasmine decides to paint a border around the walls of the bathroom. How long will the border be? Show your work.

Answer _____ feet

10 The table below shows some students' favorite lunches.

FAVORITE LUNCHES

Meal	Number of Students
Burger	6
Pizza	12
Salad	4
Taco	10
Soup	0

Part A Make a bar graph for the information in the table. Give the graph a title. Label the graph.

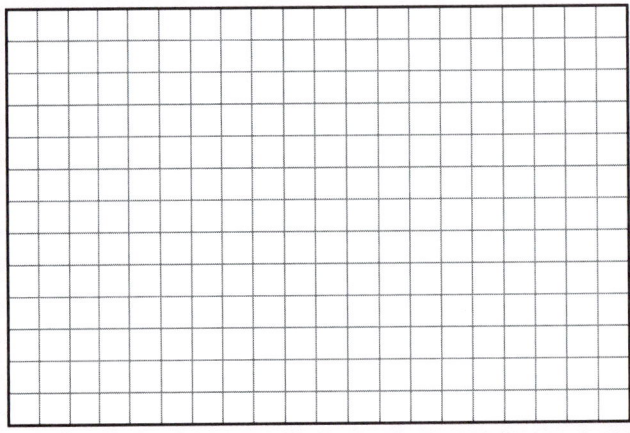

Part B Make a picture graph for the information in the table. Let the key be ◯ = 2 students. Give the picture graph a title.

Meal	Number of Students

Key: ◯ = 2 Students

284 UNIT 6 REVIEW Measurement and Data

11. This bar graph shows the number of times each number was rolled on a number cube.

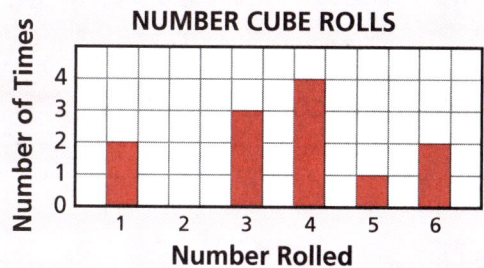

Mark True or False for each of the following statements.

	True	False
3 was rolled most often.	☐	☐
1 and 6 were rolled the same number of times.	☐	☐
2 was never rolled.	☐	☐
The number cube was rolled 10 times.	☐	☐
Either a 1 or a 3 was rolled five times.	☐	☐

12. Bala and Ernest made a banner for a basketball game. Their banner is shown below.

Part A How many square feet of fabric were used in the banner?

Answer _____ square feet

Part B Bala and Ernest trimmed the edge of the banner in white fabric tape. How many feet of tape did they need? Explain.

_____

_____

13 Mr. and Mrs. Gates put money in a savings account for each of their children on the child's birthday. Every child gets the same amount for each birthday. The bar graph shows the total amount in each child's savings account.

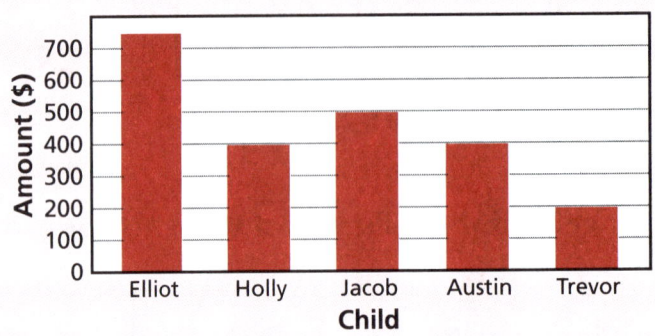

Part A Who is the oldest child in the Gates family? Explain your answer.

_____

_____

Part B How much more money does Jacob have than Trevor? Show your work.

Answer $_____

UNIT 7
Geometry

In Unit 1, you reviewed plane figures and tiling. In Unit 5, you learned how to identify and compare fractions. Now you can use what you know about fractions and plane figures to identify polygons and partition shapes using fractions.

LESSON 34 Plane Figures and Polygons In this lesson, you will draw and identify plane figures and polygons.

LESSON 35 Quadrilaterals In this lesson, you will draw and identify types of quadrilaterals, such as rectangles and rhombuses.

LESSON 36 Partitioning Shapes In this lesson, you will separate shapes into fractional pieces by dividing them into equal parts.

LESSON 34: Plane Figures and Polygons

CCLS: 3.G.1

Part 1 Introduction

A **plane figure** is a flat shape. Squares and circles are examples of plane figures.

A plane figure that is made up of **line segments** that meet is called a **polygon.** A square is a polygon. A circle is not a polygon.

Each line segment of a polygon is a **side.**
A **vertex** is the point where two sides meet.
At each vertex, there is an **angle.**

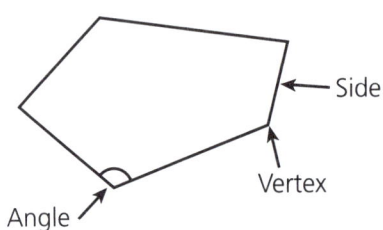

A polygon cannot be open. This is not a polygon:

You can group polygons by how they are alike or different. One way to group polygons is by the number of sides they have.

Triangle
3 sides

Quadrilateral
4 sides

Pentagon
5 sides

Hexagon
6 sides

Octagon
8 sides

What name describes this polygon?

Count the number of sides. There are 6.

This polygon is a hexagon.

288 UNIT 7 Geometry

Think About It

Name two polygons you see around you. How are they alike? How are they different?

_____

_____

 Focused Instruction

Polygons are named by the number of sides they have.

Veronica drew a figure as part of her art project. Her teacher has asked her to list all the names that describe the figure.

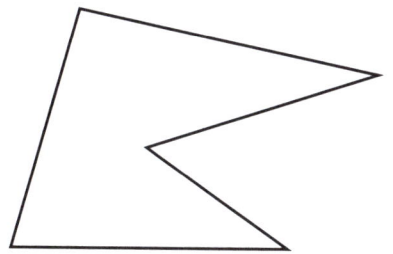

Is the figure made of only line segments? _____

Do all the line segments meet at their ends? _____

> Decide if the figure is a polygon. Then count the sides.

Is the figure a polygon? Explain.

_____

_____

How many sides does the figure have? _____

What name can you give it? _____

Focused Instruction — Lesson 34

Waldo found this picture frame in his grandmother's house.

Is the figure made of only line segments? _____

Is the figure made of line segments connected at their endpoints? _____

Is the figure a polygon? _____

How many sides does the figure have? _____

What name can you give it? _____

Use what you know about plane figures to complete this table. Mark the space for the correct name of each figure.

Figure	Triangle	Quadrilateral	Hexagon	Octagon
trapezoid				
L-shape				
M-shape				
triangle				

Guided Practice — Lesson 34

Solve the following problems.

1. What names can you use to describe the figure?

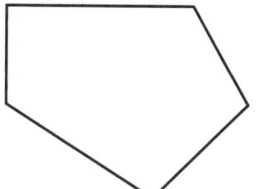

> Count the sides. Are the sides line segments?

Answer _____

2. A certain polygon has 6 vertices.

   Part A What is the name of the polygon?

   Answer _____

   > How is the number of vertices connected to the number of sides?

   Part B How many sides does the polygon have? How many angles?

   Sides _____

   Angles _____

3. Draw a polygon that has 8 angles. How many sides does it have? How many vertices?

   > Sides meet at vertices.

   Sides _____

   Vertices _____

UNIT 7 Geometry **291**

Independent Practice

Lesson 34

Solve the following problems.

1. Write the letter for each figure in the correct place in the table below.

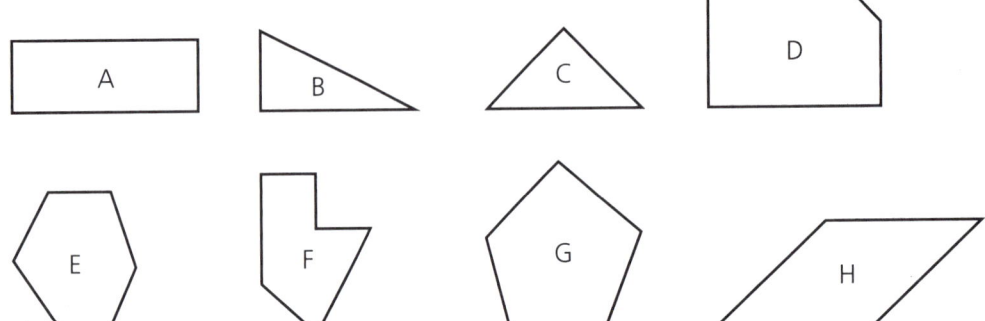

Triangle	Quadrilateral	Pentagon	Hexagon

2. Which figure below is an octagon?

A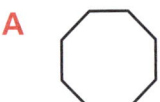

B

C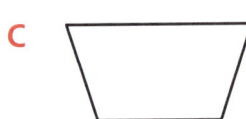

D

Independent Practice

Lesson 34

3 What type of polygon is the figure below?

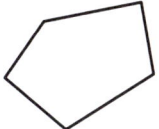

- A octagon
- B quadrilateral
- C pentagon
- D triangle

4 What is the fewest number of sides a polygon can have? Explain.

_____

_____

5 Melissa uses toothpicks to make a triangle, a quadrilateral, and a pentagon. How many toothpicks does she use in all? Explain.

_____

_____

6 Can you draw a polygon that has 5 vertices and 4 sides? Explain with a drawing.

_____

_____

_____

_____

Independent Practice — Lesson 34

7 Gil and Amit are learning about polygons in math class.

Part A Gil and Amit each drew a figure that is **not** a polygon. Explain why the figures are not polygons.

Gil's shape

Amit's shape

_____
_____
_____

Part B Gil and Amit will both draw an octagon. Gil said their octagons must look the same because they have the same number of sides. Amit said their octagons can look different. Who is correct? Explain. Draw a picture to prove you are correct.

_____
_____
_____
_____

Lesson 35: Quadrilaterals

CCLS: 3.G.1

Part 1: Introduction

A polygon with 4 sides is called a **quadrilateral.** A quadrilateral also has 4 angles and 4 vertices, or corners. Quadrilaterals can have different shapes and sizes.

One kind of quadrilateral is a **parallelogram.** The opposite sides of a parallelogram are **parallel.** That means they are always the same distance apart.

Parallelogram

A **rectangle** is a type of parallelogram. The angles of a rectangle are right angles. That means they form a square corner, or measure 90 degrees.

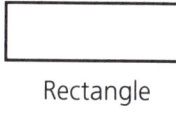
Rectangle

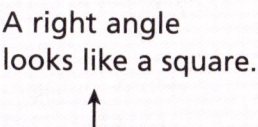
A right angle looks like a square.

A **square** is a special type of rectangle. It has 4 sides and 4 right angles. Opposite sides are parallel. All 4 sides have the same length.

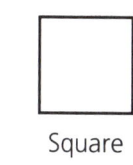
Square

A **rhombus** is a type of parallelogram. It has 4 sides that are the same length. Opposite sides are parallel. The angles in a rhombus do not have to be right angles.

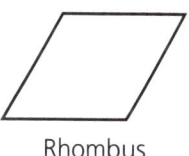
Rhombus

Some quadrilaterals do not have special names.

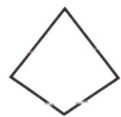  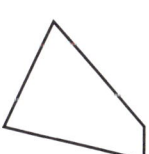 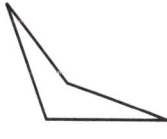

A **trapezoid** has 1 pair of parallel sides.

UNIT 7 Geometry

Think About It

Look around you. What objects do you see that are quadrilaterals? What kinds of quadrilaterals are they?

_____

_____

PART 2 Focused Instruction

Some plane figures have more than one name. First, decide if the shape is a polygon or not. Then think about the name that describes how many sides the shape has. Then think about other names that might work. Work with a partner to answer the questions.

Hera found a polished stone that looks like the shape below. She wants to give it the best name she can.

Is the shape a polygon? _____

How many sides does the shape have? _____

What is the name of a polygon with this many sides?

_____

Are opposite sides of the shape parallel? _____

What quadrilaterals have opposite sides that are parallel?

_____

_____

Measure the lengths of the sides. What do you notice?

_____

> Use a ruler to measure the lengths of the sides.

296 UNIT 7 Geometry

Focused Instruction

Lesson 35

Which quadrilaterals have 4 equal and parallel sides?

_____

Does the figure have right angles? _____

Which quadrilateral has 4 equal, parallel sides and 4 right angles? _____

What names can describe the shape?

_____

Oliver found an object that looks like this in his basement. Help Oliver identify the object.

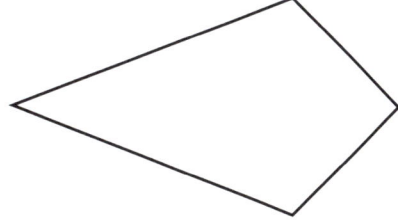

Measure the lengths of the sides. Are any of the side lengths equal? Describe them.

_____

_____

Are any of the sides parallel? _____

Are any of the corners square? _____

What name can you give this figure? _____

What real-world object does the figure look like? _____

Use what you know about quadrilaterals to identify the figures with the most specific names.

1

2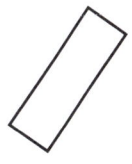

UNIT 7 Geometry

Guided Practice

Solve the following problems.

1. Lauren drew the figure below.

   Which of the following names can Lauren use to describe her figure? Circle all the names she can use.

   Polygon   Quadrilateral   Rectangle

   Square   Rhombus   Parallelogram

   First, count the number of sides. Then think about how the sides are related to each other.

2. Kyle drew a figure that has 4 sides and 4 angles. It has opposite sides parallel. It has four 4 right angles. The sides are not all the same length. What is the best name Kyle can use to describe his figure?

   Answer _____

   The best name for a figure is the most specific name for the figure.

3. Name the figure shown. Use all the names that are correct.

   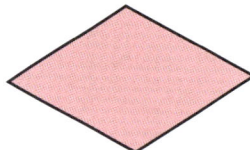

   Answer _____

   Are the sides the same length? Are the corners square?

Independent Practice

Lesson 35

Solve the following problems.

Use the figures below to answer problems 1 and 2.

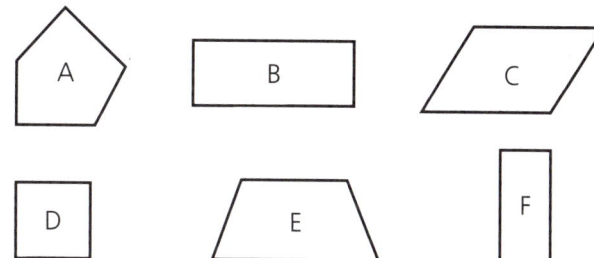

1 Write the letter of each figure in the correct place in the table below. Some shapes may go in more than one place.

Quadrilaterals	Rectangles	Not a Quadrilateral

2 Which of the following statements are true about Figure C? Select the **three** correct answers.

A It is a polygon.

B It is a quadrilateral.

C All of its sides are the same length.

D It has 4 square corners.

E It has 2 pairs of parallel sides.

3 In the space below, draw a quadrilateral. The sides of your quadrilateral should be the same length. Your quadrilateral should not have any right angles. What is the name of the quadrilateral you drew?

Answer _____

Independent Practice

4 Look at the figures below.

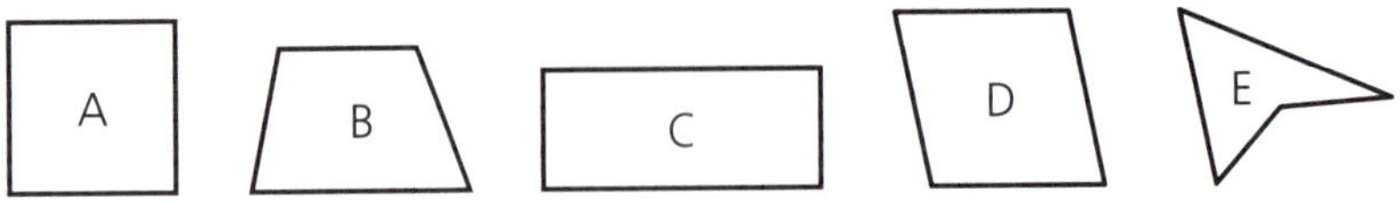

A B C D E

Which figures match this description?
- Opposite sides are parallel.
- Opposite sides are the same length.

Answer _____

5 Mark the correct place in the table to show when each of the following statements is true.

Statement	Always	Sometimes	Never
A square is a quadrilateral.			
A parallelogram is a rhombus.			
A triangle is a parallelogram.			
A rectangle is a square.			
A quadrilateral is a pentagon.			

Independent Practice

Lesson 35

6 Midori is learning how to name and group quadrilaterals based on their sides and angles.

Part A Midori needs to compare and contrast the two quadrilaterals below. Explain how the two shapes are similar and how are they different.

_____
_____
_____
_____
_____

Part B Midori says that a rhombus is never a square. Is she correct? Explain.

_____
_____
_____
_____

7 Geno says that you cannot draw a quadrilateral that has only 1 pair of parallel sides. Is he correct? Explain with drawings.

_____
_____

UNIT 7 Geometry

LESSON 36: Partitioning Shapes

Part 1 Introduction

When you divide a shape into equal parts, you **partition** it. The **area** of each part is a **unit fraction** of the whole shape.

This rectangle is divided into 2 equal parts. Each part is 1 part out of a total of 2 parts.

> A fraction with 1 for the numerator is called a **unit fraction**.

$$\frac{1}{2} \leftarrow \text{Number of parts being described}$$
$$\phantom{\frac{1}{2}} \leftarrow \text{Number of equal parts}$$

> The top number in a fraction is the **numerator**. The bottom number is the **denominator**.

That means each part is one half, or $\frac{1}{2}$, of the area of the whole shape.

To use unit fractions to describe the area, the parts must be the same size.

Each part of this circle is $\frac{1}{4}$ of the area of the total circle.

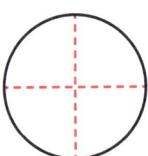

This circle does not have parts that are the same size. So one part is not $\frac{1}{4}$ of the area of the entire circle.

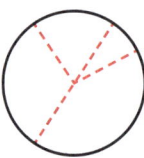

Think About It

Describe something at home that you might partition. Consider ways you might partition food, closets, or rooms.

_____

_____

Focused Instruction — Lesson 36

Counters or tiles can help you understand partitioning a shape. Use counters or tiles with the rectangle below or create another rectangle out of 6 counters.

Partition the rectangle into 6 equal parts.

[rectangle]

Fill in the fraction to show the area of one part of the rectangle.

☐ ← Each part
――
☐ ← Total parts

What unit fraction describes the area of each part? _____

Is there another way you can partition this shape into 6 equal parts? Explain.

_____
_____

Focused Instruction

Lesson 36

Shapes are not always partitioned into squares. An octagon can be partitioned into triangles.

Look at the octagon below.

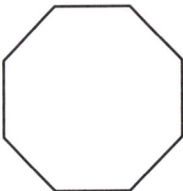

> Think of each side as the bottom of a triangle.

Draw lines to make 8 equal parts in the octagon.

Fill in the fraction to show the area of one part of the octagon.

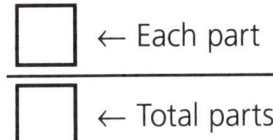

What unit fraction describes the area of each part of the octagon? _____

Use what you know about partitioning figures to write a fraction to describe the area of each part of these figures.

1.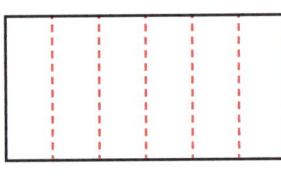

   _____

2.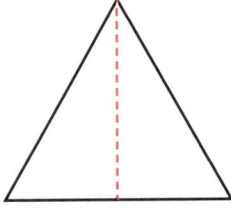

   _____

Guided Practice

Lesson 36

Solve the following problems.

1. Partition the circle so each part is $\frac{1}{2}$ of the area of the entire circle.

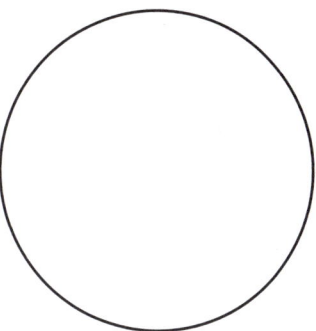

Remember that there can be more than one way to partition a figure.

2. Partition the square below so that each part has an area that is $\frac{1}{8}$ of the area of the whole square.

If each section is $\frac{1}{8}$ of the total area, how many sections are there?

UNIT 7 Geometry

Independent Practice

Lesson 36

Solve the following problems.

1. What unit fraction describes the area of each part of the circle?

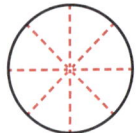

   A $\frac{1}{4}$

   B $\frac{1}{2}$

   C $\frac{1}{8}$

   D $\frac{1}{6}$

2. Which square is divided into parts that are $\frac{1}{6}$ of the area of the whole square? Select the **two** correct answers.

   A

   B

   C

   D

   E

   F

306 UNIT 7 Geometry

© The Continental Press, Inc. DUPLICATING THIS MATERIAL IS ILLEGAL.

Independent Practice — Lesson 36

3 Francesca says that each part of this circle is $\frac{1}{6}$ of the area of the whole circle. Brent says that each part is $\frac{1}{3}$ of the area of the whole circle. Who is correct? Explain.

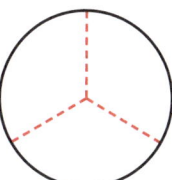

_____

_____

4 Drew tried to partition an octagon so that each part was $\frac{1}{4}$ of the area of the whole octagon. What did he do wrong? Explain.

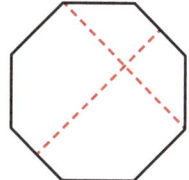

_____

_____

Independent Practice

Lesson 36

5 June organized her desk drawers. She used dividers to make sections in a drawer.

Part A June wanted to create 8 sections in one drawer. She wanted each section to have the same area. Partition the rectangles below in 2 different ways to show how June could have divided her desk drawer into 8 equal sections.

Part B If June decided to keep paper clips in 1 section of the desk drawer, what fraction of the area of the desk drawer will hold paper clips?

Answer _____

UNIT 7 REVIEW
Geometry

CCLS: 3.G.1, 2

Solve the following problems.

1. Which figure below is a polygon?

   A

   B

   C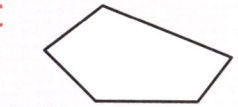

   D

2. How many sides does an octagon have?

   A 4

   B 5

   C 6

   D 8

3. What fraction of the square's area is each part?

   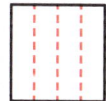

   Answer _____

4 A parallelogram has all sides the same length and 4 right angles. What is its name?

  A rhombus

  B triangle

  C rectangle

  D square

5 Zhu made two groups of quadrilaterals. The first group has quadrilaterals with angles that are all equal. The second group has quadrilaterals with sides that are equal. Which quadrilateral does Zhu **not** have in either of his groups?

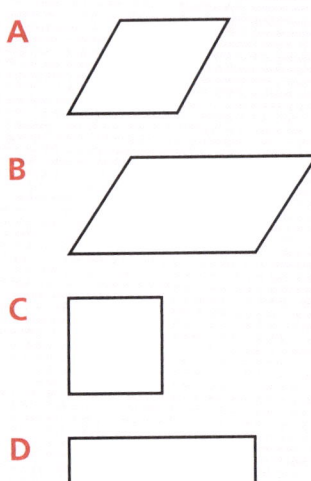

  A

  B

  C

  D

6 Derrick drew a shape. The shape is a 4-sided figure with angles that are not all the same size. Which shape could Derrick have drawn? Select the **three** correct answers.

  A rhombus

  B rectangle

  C square

  D quadrilateral

  E triangle

  F parallelogram

7 Which circle is divided into parts that are each $\frac{1}{3}$ of the area of the entire circle?

A

B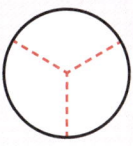

C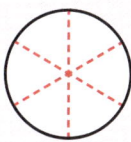

D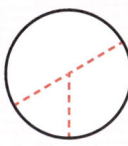

8 Cassidy drew a polygon with 6 sides. What is the name of the polygon that Cassidy drew?

Answer _____

9 Look at the figure below.

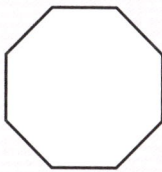

Part A What is the name of this figure?

Answer _____

Part B Divide the figure into equal parts. What fraction of the whole area is each part?

Answer _____

10 Look at the shapes below.

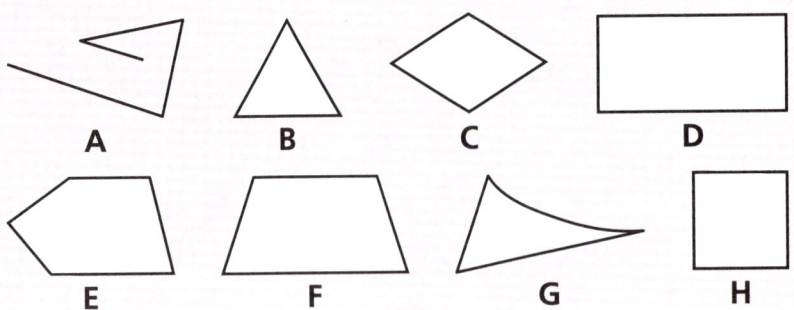

Part A Which of these figures are polygons? Explain.

_____
_____
_____

Part B Which of these figures are parallelograms? Explain.

_____
_____
_____

11 Leslie partitioned the parallelogram below.

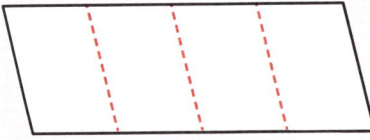

Part A What unit fraction describes each part?

Answer _____

Part B How could Leslie draw one more line to partition the parallelogram so that each part is $\frac{1}{8}$ of the area of the whole parallelogram? Explain.

_____
_____
_____
_____

12 Draw a quadrilateral that is not a parallelogram.

13 Consider the quadrilaterals shown.

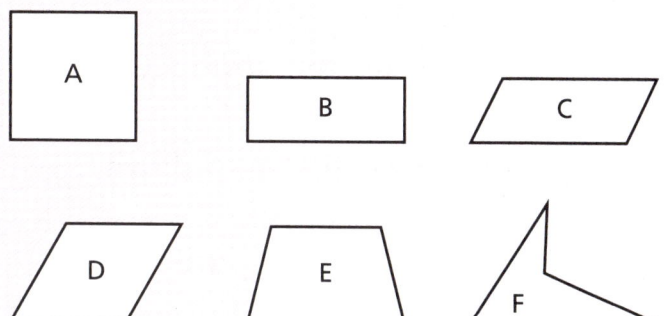

Part A List the figures for each category. Some shapes may go in more than one place.

4 Right Angles	Both Opposite Sides Parallel	No Right Angles

Part B Classify each quadrilateral using the word box. Write the best name for each figure.

Quadrilateral   Rectangle   Square   Rhombus   Trapezoid   Parallelogram

Figure A _____

Figure B _____

Figure C _____

Figure D _____

Figure E _____

Figure F _____

GLOSSARY

A

add: to put together

addends: numbers that are added in an addition problem to find a sum

addition table: a table that shows the sums of all combinations of one-digit numbers

angle: a figure formed by two rays that share an endpoint and extend in different directions

area: the amount of space inside a figure, measured in square units. The area formula for a rectangle is Area = length × width.

array: a model using rows and columns of symbols or shapes

associative property: allows grouping of numbers with parentheses to be added or multiplied: $a + (b + c) = (a + b) + c$ and $a \times (b \times c) = (a \times b) \times c$

B

bar graph: a data display that uses bars to show data

C

capacity: the measure of how much liquid something holds; also called *liquid volume*

centimeter: a small unit of length in the metric system. A centimeter is about the width of a finger.

clock: a tool used to tell time

commutative property: allows numbers to be added or multiplied in any order: $a + b = b + a$ and $a \times b = b \times a$

compare: to decide which number is greater than or less than another number

customary system: a system of measurement used in the United States. It measures length using inches, feet, yards, and miles.

D

data: information

denominator: the number of parts in a whole or set, the number on the bottom of a fraction

difference: the answer in a subtraction problem

distributive property: allows a number to be multiplied by a sum or each addend to be multiplied separately and the products added: $a(b + c) = ab + ac$

divide: to split a group into smaller groups of equal size

dividend: the number being divided in a division problem

divisor: the number doing the dividing in a division problem

E

elapsed time: the amount of time that passes from the start time of an event to the end time; also called *time interval*

equation: a number sentence that says two expressions are equal

equivalent: equal to

estimate: to decide about how much or how many; to make a good guess

expression: a grouping of numbers and operations that shows the value of something

F

fact family: a set of four related multiplication and division number sentences for three numbers

factors: whole numbers that multiply to form a product

fraction: a way of showing parts of a whole or of a set; shown as the number of parts being discussed over the total number of equal parts ($\frac{1}{2}, \frac{3}{4}$)

foot: a medium unit of length in the customary system. There are 12 inches in 1 foot.

G

gram: a small unit of mass in the metric system

H

hexagon: a polygon with six sides

hour: a unit of time. There are 24 hours in 1 day.

hour hand: the short hand on a clock; points to the hour

I

identity property: states that any number multiplied by 1 is always that number; any number divided by 1 is always that number

inch: a small unit of length in the customary system; about the length of a paper clip

inverse operations: operations that undo each other, opposite operations. Addition and subtraction are inverse operation. Multiplication and division are inverse operations.

K

kilogram: a large unit of mass in the metric system. There are 1,000 grams in 1 kilogram.

L

length: the measure of how long something is

line plot: a plot in which data is represented by Xs placed over a number line; also called a dot plot

line segments: parts of a line that make up the sides of figures

liter: a unit of capacity in the metric system

M

mass: a measure of how heavy something is in metric units

meter: a unit of length in the metric system. There are 100 centimeters in 1 meter.

metric system: a system of measurement used in most of the world. It includes units of

- capacity—milliliter, liter
- mass—gram, kilogram

minute: a unit of time. There are 60 minutes in 1 hour.

minute hand: the long hand on a clock; points to the minute

multiples: the products of a number and nonzero whole numbers

multiplication table: a table that shows the products of all combinations of one-digit numbers

multiply: to combine groups of equal size

N **number line:** a line that shows a set of ordered numbers, represented by tick marks

numerator: the number of parts talked about, the number on the top of a fraction

O **octagon:** a polygon with eight sides

P **parallel:** describes sides that are always the same distance apart and do not meet

parallelogram: a quadrilateral with two pairs of parallel sides

parentheses: grouping symbols used to show order in a number sentence. Always do the operation inside parentheses first.

partition: to divide or split

pattern: a sequence that follows a set rule

pentagon: a polygon with five sides

perimeter: the distance around a figure

picture graph: a data display that uses pictures or symbols to show information

place value: the value of a digit in a number based on where it is located in the number

plane figure: a flat shape

polygon: a two-dimensional figure with line segments for sides

product: the answer in a multiplication problem

Q **quadrilateral:** a polygon with four sides

quotient: the answer in a division problem

R **rectangle:** a parallelogram with four right angles

regroup: to exchange 1 in one place for 10 in the place to its right, or 10 in one place for 1 in the place to its left; example: 2 tens can be regrouped as 1 ten and 10 ones

regular polygon: a polygon in which all the sides are the same length and all the angles are the same size

repeated addition: a way of showing multiplication by adding the same number multiple times (3 × 4 = 4 + 4 + 4)

repeated subtraction: a way of showing division by subtracting the same number multiple times (20 − 5 − 5 − 5 − 5 = 0, so 20 ÷ 5 = 4)

rhombus: a parallelogram with four equal sides

round: to replace a number with a close number that tells about how many or how much

ruler: a tool used to measure length

S

scale: the numbers on a graph

side: a line segment that forms part of a polygon

square: a rectangle with four equal sides

square unit: a unit of measure for area that is 1 unit long and 1 unit wide, such as square inches, square centimeters, or square meters

subtract: to take away

sum: the answer in an addition problem

symbol: a small picture that stands for something

T

tally chart: a data display that shows data using tallies, or slashes

tally mark: a slash on a tally chart that represents 1 thing or 1 time

tiling: a way of finding the area of a figure by covering it with unit squares

trapezoid: a quadrilateral with exactly one pair of parallel sides

triangle: a polygon with three sides

U

unit fraction: a fraction with a numerator of 1

V

vertex: the place where two sides of a polygon meet; the endpoint shared by two rays that form an angle

volume: the measure of the amount of space something takes up

Y **yard:** a unit of length in the customary system. There are 3 feet in 1 yard.

Z **zero property:** states that any number multiplied by 0 is always 0; 0 divided by any number is always 0; no number can be divided by 0

3 ↑ × 4 ↑ = 12	3 × 4 = 12 ↑
3)¯18̄ ⁶ ←	→ 3)¯18̄ ⁶
3)¯18̄ ⁶ ←	3 × 5 = 5 × 3
2 × (3 × 5) = (2 × 3) × 5	$\frac{1}{2}$ ←

product	factors
divisor	dividend
commutative property of multiplication	quotient
numerator	associative property of multiplication

→ $\frac{1}{2}$ $3(2+4) = (3 \times 2) + (3 \times 4)$

distributive property

denominator

square

rectangle

triangle

parallelogram

trapezoid

rhombus

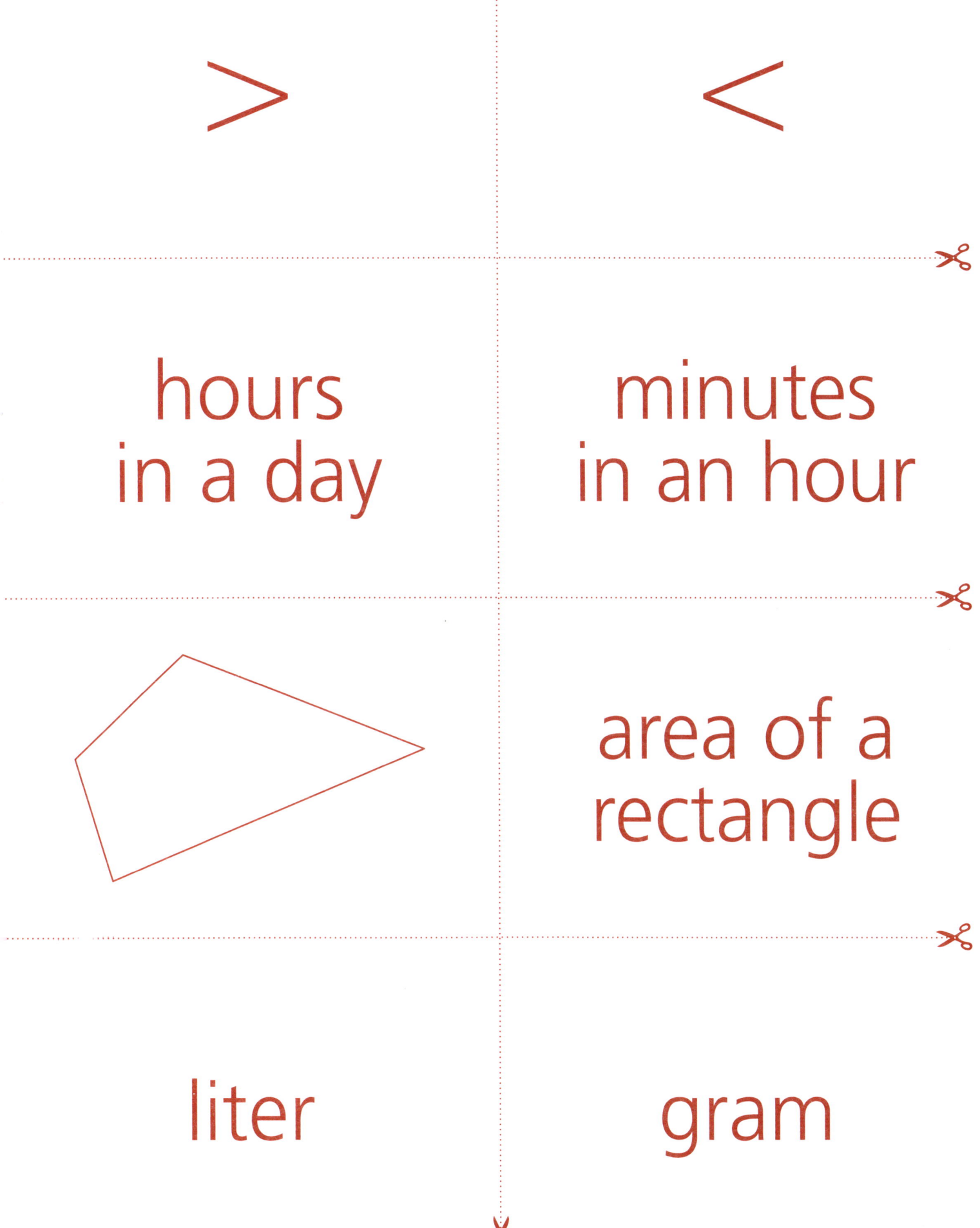

| is less than symbol | is greater than symbol |

| 60 | 24 |

| Area = length × width $A = l \times w$ | quadrilateral |

| unit of mass | unit of capacity |

kilogram

unit of mass